The Nez Perces:
The History of Their Troubles
and the Campaign of 1877

by Duncan McDonald

Duncan McDonald

The Nez Perces:
The History of Their Troubles and the Campaign of 1877

by Duncan McDonald

edited by
Robert Bigart
and
Joseph McDonald

published by
Salish Kootenai College Press
Pablo, Montana

distributed by
University of Nebraska Press
Lincoln, Nebraska

2016

Cover illustrations: Front cover top: Duncan McDonald, 943-624, Montana Historical Society Photograph Archives, Helena. Front cover bottom: Chief Looking Glass, National Anthropological Archives, Smithsonian Institution Washington, D.C., inv. 01005001, photo lot 4420, photo by William Henry Jackson, 1871. Back cover: Chief Joseph, standing, Library of Congress, Photograph Division, Washington, D.C., USZ 61-2086.
  Frontispiece: Duncan McDonald, 943-624, Montana Historical Society Photograph Archives, Helena.

Library of Congress Cataloging-in-Publication Data:
Names: McDonald, Duncan, author. | Bigart, Robert, editor. | McDonald, Joseph, 1933- editor.
Title: The Nez Perces: the history of their troubles and the Campaign of 1877 / by Duncan McDonald ; edited by Robert Bigart and Joseph McDonald.
Description: Pablo, Montana : Salish Kootenai College Press, 2016. | Includes biographical references and index.
Identifiers: LCCN 2016004247 | ISBN 9781934594162
Subjects: LCSH: Nez Perce Indians--Wars, 1877.
Classification: LCC E83.877 .M28 2016 | DDC 979.5004/974124--dc23
LC record available at http://lccn.loc.gov/2016004247

Distributed by University of Nebraska Press, 1111 Lincoln Mall, Lincoln, NE 68588-0630, order 1-800-755-1105, www.nebraskapress.unl.edu.

Table of Contents

Flathead Indian Reservation
Showing Tribal Territories and Surrounding Towns

Map by Marcia Bakry, Smithsonian Institution, Washington, D.C., 1973

Introduction:
Duncan McDonald, 1849-1937

by Joseph McDonald

Duncan McDonald was a very influential person in his lifetime. He stood up often for the rights of the American Indians. He was a successful businessman, historian, and writer, and had boundless energy. He served as a liaison between the tribal community and white settlers and government officials and elucidated the American Indian side of an issue. He was held in high esteem by my aunts, uncles, and cousins. I heard about many of his feats and accomplishments as I was growing up.

Duncan was born in 1849 at the Ft. Connah Trading Post. His mother, Catherine, and his father, Angus, were living at the post, and Angus was in charge of its operation. Catherine delivered her babies by herself. She believed they grew up much stronger than if she had assistance. Duncan grew up a very strong man. His mother was a great teacher and strong in her Nez Perce culture. His father, Angus, preferred the Indian way of life to that of the white people that were coming west. Duncan had an interesting childhood and took a particular interest in the cultural practices of Indians.

In a 1929 interview by William S. Lewis, Duncan told Lewis that he viewed himself with "Indian eyes."[1] He felt that most white people saw him as Indian although his father was pure Scotch blood. Angus was a descendant from the strain of

McDonalds that escaped from Glencoe, Scotland, when English King William's troops attempted to kill the entire clan.

Duncan was proud of his Indian culture and was a protector of Indian civil and human rights, and was a successful business entrepreneur.

His mother preferred living in a tepee and raising her family in the tepee. The fort had a residence building, but she did not use it. Duncan grew up there and at Ft. Colville in what is now eastern Washington. During the winter months his father always provided a schoolteacher for the family. Duncan grew up learning to read, write, and do numbers. He said that they also learned some lessons from the clerks who all had some education.

At age 19 he became the manager of the Ft. Connah Trading Post while his father was the Chief Trader for the Hudson's Bay Company (HBC) and worked out of Ft. Colville. The HBC was closing out its operations in the United States in the late 1860s and early 1870s, and Duncan was put in charge of closing Ft. Connah. Business had been declining at the trading post for a number of reasons. The St. Ignatius Mission was becoming more developed and provided the Indian people some of their needs. Also the Mullan Road had been completed connecting western Montana with Idaho and thus taking some of the travelers on a route that did not pass by the fort. The Hudson's Bay Company was going through hearings with the United States as to the value of its holdings below the forty ninth parallel. An agreement was reached in 1872 and the fort closed as a Hudson's Bay trading post.

Angus reached a land use agreement with the Salish and Pend d'Oreille leaders and made his home at the site of the Ft. Connah Trading Post, where he raised the younger children of his family. It is said that Duncan had a two story log home built that served as Angus' and Catherine's home until they both passed away.

After closing out the trading post, Duncan went directly into the retail business and established a well managed store near the Jocko Agency. He later developed a restaurant and rooming business at the Ravalli train station. People got off the train at Ravalli and patronized his businesses while waiting for the Allard Stage to take them up into the Mission Valley. He also had a ranch operation and a large apple orchard down river from Ravalli. He was always involved in some entrepreneurial activity. He bought flour and shipped it to mining camps in Canada, and he was an avid prospector for gold.

There was a prominent rock apple cellar nestled into the hillside at the foot of Ravalli Hill. It was removed when the highway was widened a few years ago. It was constructed well enough that not long ago a family made it into a temporary home while building their restaurant that is now the Bison Cafe. Duncan's restaurant building at Ravalli has been moved to the Four Winds Trading Post north of St. Ignatius.

Later he built a family home in Dixon. It was across the railroad tracks and on the way to the river. Mary Catherine "Sis" McDonald and her husband Jim Swaney lived across the road from his home. In his elder years, he rented out the house and lived in a cabin in the back of the house. This is where he lived when he died. He died at Thompson Falls. Family members say that he was at Thompson Falls, the county seat, to start the eviction of his renters who he felt were not living up to their agreement with him.

Family members, such as my aunt, Florence Smith, said he lost most of his wealth in the hard winters that hit the area in 1927 – 1928. His cattle died in the cold and his apple orchard had extensive frost damage. He lost most of his savings when the bank where he had deposited his money closed.

In the prime of his life, Duncan had many notable accomplishments. From 1867 until into the 1930s he managed a number of different businesses. He served as a liaison or cultural broker between the American Indian people and the white people pouring into the country. He spoke several Indian languages as well as sign language. He was a good writer. He was active in politics, visited with writers, developed businesses, and climbed mountains. On one of his mountain trips, he carved his name at the outlet of a large lake on the west side of Glacier Park. The lake was later named Lake McDonald because of the tree he put his name on.

His first experience in business management began when he took over the trading activities at Fort Connah. He traded with the Indians and the fur trappers. He priced the products being brought to the trading post which included buffalo hides and hides of beaver, marten, muskrats, ermine, wolves, and coyotes. He also traded for buffalo hair ropes, rawhide ropes, buffalo tallow, pemmican, dried meat, and horse accouterments. In the spring of the year, everything that was purchased during the winter was shipped to Fort Colville by packhorse. The packhorses brought trade goods back to Fort Connah. This same procedure occurred in the fall.

He continually wrote and spoke in support of the Indians in disputes with the white society. He had a way of explaining the Indian side of an issue. His opinions were well received and respected.

Duncan served as a historian of the Nez Perce War. His mother's family was closely related to many Nez Perce who were on the retreat through Montana. He paid close attention to their movements and interviewed survivors to compose a history of the Nez Perce side of the 1877 war for the *New North-West* newspaper that was published in Deer Lodge, Montana. He also visited regularly with the *Weekly Missoulian*, which was published in Missoula, Montana. In 1878 the *New North-West* notified its readers that it was going to publish a series of articles about Joseph's 1877 campaign. It went on to say that Duncan McDonald, a relative of Looking Glass, would be the author and it was the condition of the publication that the views expressed in the history be from an Indian's standpoint. It was intended to give a history of the course of the outbreak, Joseph's battles, and his historic march through the mountains.

Growing up, I heard so many stories about Duncan's travel feats on horseback. He explored the Mission Mountains thoroughly and rode his horse into mountain lakes and passes that are difficult to access on foot. I was a small boy (4 years old) when I saw him outside of his little one room cabin. The cabin sat behind his nice home. He died a relatively poor man with little money and hardly any personal assets, but he was rich in cultural and political history. He had no surviving immediate family. His son and daughter died young and he had no grandchildren. He is buried beneath the Mission Mountains in the St. Ignatius Catholic Cemetery alongside his wife Louise, his son Col, and his daughter Mary.

The following pages are dedicated to his life.

Joe McDonald
Grand Nephew

Duncan McDonald:
Nez Perce War Historian, 1877-1880

by Robert Bigart and Joseph McDonald

The rumbles of war between the Nez Perce Indians and the United States Army in Idaho in 1877 set Duncan on a trajectory emphasizing his growing role as a cultural broker. Duncan's prominence as mediator between the Indian and white communities in western Montana made him a familiar and respected public figure, but also raised the risk he faced if the white community suspected him of supporting the Nez Perce who were fighting the U.S. Army — and some of the belligerents were his relatives.

The hostile Nez Perce heading west over the Lolo Trail during summer 1877 created serious problems for those Nez Perce who wanted to stay out of the war. For example, one Nez Perce chief who opposed the war, Eagle-of-the-Light, arrived at Flathead Agency in 1877. His band camped near Chief Arlee's home at Jocko for the duration of the war. The eleven lodges in his band professed their neutrality and friendship towards the white settlers, and they survived the hostilities safely.[1]

Since Duncan was half Nez Perce and half white, he was suspect in the eyes of some white Montanans. Indian runners conveyed word of the outbreak of hostilities to the Montana tribes, and Duncan relayed the news to Montana newspapers.[2] Especially risky for Duncan were rumors circulating in Missoula that he had sold ammunition to hostile Nez Perce warriors at his Jocko Agency trading post. Duncan related the story in his Nez Perce War history. Three Nez Perce were working as scouts for General Nelson Miles against Sitting Bull and the Sioux. When they learned that war had broken out in Idaho, they deserted Miles and attempted to get home to their families. They reached the Jocko Agency and learned that the hostile Nez Perce were on the Lolo Trail. The three men had a pack mule, but Duncan insisted it was "for their blankets and cooking utensils and not to pack cartridges." When the three found they could not reach their homes via Horse Plains, they returned to the Jocko Agency. Duncan advised Grizzly Bear Youth, the leader of the group, to go to Lolo and surrender to General O. O. Howard in order to keep out of the war. But when the three Nez Perce reached the Bitterroot Valley, they entered the Nez Perce camp and advised Looking Glass and White Bird to head north through the Flathead Reservation to Canada. Looking Glass and the hostile Nez Perce decided instead to head for the Yellowstone Valley where they could join the Crow Indians.[3]

Duncan's later description of his personal activities while the hostile Nez Perce were passing through Montana was a bit vague. On February 1, 1928, he wrote Lucullus V. McWhorter that, when the Nez Perce came down the Lolo Trail in late July 1877, he tried but failed to enter the hostile camp:

> I was about four miles West of Missoula when I met the volunteers going back to Missoula. I asked them where are the hostiles? They told me that they are out of the LoLo or Capt Rawns Fort an[d] moved up the Bitter Root Valley. In getting this information I changed my notion and returned to Missoula. I was calculating to go right into the hostile camp, since they got out LoLo, I quit.

He did not explain what he had intended to do if he reached the camp of the hostile Nez Perce before they entered the Bitterroot Valley. Duncan said he was home at Jocko Agency while the Battle of the Big Hole was being fought in August 1877.[4]

Duncan may have had more contact with the Nez Perce hostiles in 1877 than he wanted to admit publicly in later years. Both a McDonald family oral tradition and a Nez Perce tribal historian indicated Duncan met with the Nez Perce hostiles in

western Montana and encouraged them to head north through
western Montana to reach safety in Canada. In one source, Camille Williams, the Nez Perce historian, indicated that Duncan's
father Angus sent Duncan to the Nez Perce camp to get them
to head north rather than east to Crow country. According to
Williams, Angus wanted Duncan to "lead them to Canada, as
Duncan knew the trail."[5] Despite any pleadings by Duncan,
Chief Looking Glass and the Nez Perce hostiles continued on to
Crow country.

After the Nez Perce left the Bitterroot Valley, they were engaged in a series of battles with the United States Army. Loss of
Nez Perce life and property was especially severe in the Battle
of the Big Hole in southwest Montana in August 1877. In late
September 1877, the Nez Perce were surrounded and attacked at
the Bear Paw Mountains, just forty miles from safety in Canada.
Chief Joseph and most of the Nez Perce surrendered and were
taken to Kansas as prisoners of war. More than 200 Nez Perce
refugees from the last battle escaped and fled north over the border. The Nez Perce refugees in Canada were led by Chief White
Bird, whom Duncan later interviewed for his history of the Nez
Perce War.[6]

According to Duncan's February 1, 1928, letter to Mc-
Whorter, the editor of the *New North-West* newspaper in Deer
Lodge, James Mills, asked him to write the history:

I was asked by Cap James Mills who was publishing the
New North West in Deer Lodge he wanted to write up
the cause of the war from the Indian point of view and
by asking who he could get the information from Indian
side. By inquiring he was told to give the job to Duncan McDonald being on the Flathead Indian reservation.
This man is the writer.[7]

Duncan's father, Angus, wrote that Duncan had showed his
father "the invitation to do it," and Angus gave Duncan his "views
as to how it should be done but that [it] required more time and
means than he had." Duncan "started to write them without my
knowledge." Angus said the installments were "written originally

by Duncan and then prepared somewhat by Baird & Gregg."
Angus said he suggested Duncan delay some of the publication
for a while, because "the Country [was] now too sore about the
Nez Perces at least I think so." Some of the publication coincided
with the 1878 murder of three Philipsburg area miners by Nez
Perce warriors returning to Idaho after the war.[8]

The two white men Angus identified as helping Duncan
with the Nez Perce War history were Robert McGregor Baird
and Omar G. V. Gregg. Baird had been Duncan's prospecting
companion in 1876. He was a former school teacher in Missoula
and by 1877 was in charge of T. J. Demers' businesses at French-
town. In the early 1880s he was Flathead Indian Agency clerk,
and in the 1880 United States census he gave his occupation as
"bohemian." In 1884 Baird was murdered by a white man in the
British Columbia Kootenai country while taking a pack train to
the Kootenai Valley for T. J. Demers.[9]

Gregg was a Confederate Civil War veteran who worked
at various Montana newspapers in the late nineteenth century.
In 1876 and 1877, he was employed by the St. Ignatius Mission print shop publishing Salish language books. In March and
April of 1878 he wrote several letters to area newspapers complaining about the use of flogging by Flathead Reservation chiefs.
That same year, he was a justice of the peace in Missoula. At the
turn of the century, he was a forest ranger in the Flathead forest reserve.[10] Exactly what Angus meant when he wrote that the
manuscript was "prepared somewhat by Baird & Gregg" and the
extent of their editorial changes is not known.

James H. Mills, the editor of the *New North-West* newspaper in Deer Lodge between 1869 and 1891, was an exceptional
man. For a newspaperman in 1878 Montana to seek out and
support the publication of the Indian side of the 1877 Nez Perce
War was remarkable. Mills was born in Ohio in 1837. He served
in the United States Army between 1861 and 1864 and reached
the rank of a brevet lieutenant colonel. Soon after he was mus-
tered out of the army, he engaged in a mining enterprise in the
Yellowstone Valley. He and his partners gave their money to a

packer who was to purchase supplies for them in Bozeman. After the packer gambled away the supply money, the miners were broke and had to abandon their claim. Mills arrived at Virginia City with ten cents in capital. In 1866, he was offered the job as editor of the *Montana Post*, the first newspaper in Montana Territory. He continued at the *Montana Post* in Virginia City and later Helena until the newspaper ceased publication in 1869. Between 1869 and 1891, he was editor of the *New North-West* newspaper in Deer Lodge. From 1877 through 1879, he was also secretary of Montana Territory. After 1891, he held various political offices in Montana. He died in 1904.[11]

Mills announced the new series about the Nez Perce campaign in the April 19, 1878, issue of the *New North-West*. In explaining the need for the history, Mills stated, "The Red Man's side of the story has not yet been told." Mills asked Duncan to write the history because Duncan was "probably the best informed upon the subject to be written up of any one in Montana." Mills "requested that the story be told as the Nez Perces know it, regardless of the views of the whites, and hope to present an account of interest and value."[12]

The first installment of "The Nez Perces: The History of Their Troubles and the Campaign of 1877," by Duncan McDonald, "a relative of Looking Glass and White Bird," appeared in the April 26, 1878, issue. The introduction noted that, "It is a condition of the publication that the views shall be related from their standpoint, and as full particulars as possible will be given of the tribe and their great expedition."[13]

Almost as surprising at Mills' interest in publishing the Indian side of the story in 1878 was that some other Montana newspapers gave approving notices of the history. One newspaper observed that the series seems "to be a plain concise statement, and perhaps contains 'more truth than poetry,'" Another paper observed that Duncan's articles "promise to be very interesting reading." The *Benton Record* at Fort Benton, Montana, observed Duncan "no doubt will give only the Nez Perces view of the subject; but that is more likely to be a correct version of the troubles and adventures of the tribe than were the reports of the army officers who were out-generaled by Chief Joseph."[14]

On June 14, 1878, the *New North-West* announced that the publication of the Nez Perce War series was being suspended so Duncan could travel to Canada to interview the Nez Perce refugees living there. Duncan submitted a general article outlining the Indian history of white oppression and betrayal. He particularly complained about a Montana Territory law that prohibited Indians, blacks, and Chinese from testifying against white persons in court: "In a country which holds these horrible sentiments true civilization and what is worth anything of that much prostituted term, Christianity, are of non-effect." The whites had repeatedly forced land cessions on the tribes and refused to punish white criminals who murdered Indians. (Mills added a note that while the provision prohibiting Indian and other testimony against white men in court had been approved in 1864, it had been discarded when the criminal code was revised in 1872.)[15]

In middle June 1878, Duncan departed on his trip to Canada to interview White Bird in the Cypress Hills. On June 12 he "was nearly killed by a horse" and was crippled but still expected to reach White Bird's camp.[16] On June 18, 1878, Duncan passed through Helena.[17]

Before Duncan reached the Dearborn River, he met a Pend d'Oreille Indian traveling with a Nez Perce couple. They nearly encountered a Nez Perce war party that stole 140 horses on the Sun River. Duncan and his companions were captured by the Gros Ventre Indians when they reached the Milk River. Duncan protested that he was on official business for the Montana Territory Secretary, James H. Mills, and the Gros Ventre released them.[18]

Duncan made it to Canada and neared Fort Walsh, the Canadian Mounted Police post north of Havre. He met Col. Acheson Irvine, the Canadian police commander at Fort Walsh, who was also on his way to White Bird's camp. Irvine wanted to convince White Bird to meet First Lieutenant George W. Baird of the United States Army, who had traveled to Fort Walsh to negotiate with White Bird. Duncan and Irvine had met before in 1875 when Duncan was on a trading expedition to the area. When Irvine learned they were both headed for White Bird's camp and Duncan was part Nez Perce, he solicited Duncan to be his interpreter. The United States Army had received intelligence that White Bird wanted to surrender and return to the United States, but White Bird was apparently surprised at the news that a United States Army officer was at Fort Walsh to talk about surrender. When Duncan and Col. Irvine of the Canadian police located the Nez Perce camp, they headed for White Bird's lodge. The Nez Perce feared Irvine would attempt to arrest White Bird and forcibly return him to the United States. They crowded into the lodge to protect White Bird if needed. Irvine and Duncan introduced themselves but did not mention the purpose of their visit at their first meeting.

Later Irvine explained his mission was to have White Bird come to Fort Walsh and meet with Lt. Baird. Most of the Sioux and Nez Perce feared that, despite Col. Irvine's promise of safe conduct, White Bird would be arrested if he went to Fort Walsh. The negotiations were tense and some accused Duncan of being a spy for the United States government. Finally White Bird asked Duncan, "Are you telling me the truth? Do you think there is any danger going to Fort Walsh?" Duncan assured White Bird that Lt. Baird only wanted to talk to White Bird. After three days of indecision, White Bird finally agreed to accompany Irvine, Duncan, and the police to Fort Walsh.

At Fort Walsh the conference between White Bird, Lt. Baird of the United States Army, and Col. Irvine and Commissioner James Macleod of the Canadian police commenced on July 1, 1878, with Duncan serving as interpreter. White Bird stated he would only surrender if the United States government respected General Nelson Miles' 1877 promise and allowed Chief Joseph and the Nez Perce prisoners to return to Idaho.

Lt. Baird countered with an argument that if White Bird surrendered and joined Joseph in exile, it was "very likely" that the government would then allow all the Nez Perce to return to their homeland. Baird threatened White Bird, that, if White Bird did not surrender, then Joseph "will probably never be sent back." Then White Bird offered to surrender if Baird promised in front of witnesses that he and Joseph would be allowed to return to Idaho. Baird replied, "I cant promise that," and White Bird refused to leave his Canadian refuge.

When White Bird and Duncan returned to the Nez Perce camp, Duncan learned that the Indians at the camp had promised that, "If White Bird dont return, we will kill Duncan McDonald." On July 2, 1878, Duncan wrote editor Mills that White Bird had refused to surrender.[19] Duncan did, however, get his interview with White Bird about the events of the 1877 Nez Perce War.

When Duncan returned to Fort Walsh after the interview, he found Neptune Lynch selling horses. Lynch was one of the early white settlers at Horse Plains, west of the Flathead Reservation, and a legendary horse trader and trainer.[20] Duncan went home to Montana accompanied by a young Salish woman he had found living in White Bird's camp who wanted to return to the Flathead Reservation. He had planned to stop at Deer Lodge on his way back from Canada, but his horses were so worn out that he decided to return directly to Jocko.[21]

On July 26, 1878, Mills wrote in the *New North-West* that Duncan had arrived safely at Jocko Agency after a six week trip. Duncan had spent ten days interviewing White Bird: "White Bird's story was very interesting." The note promised Duncan's series of papers would "be resumed shortly...and we doubt not that [the] interested attention they have attracted will be fully maintained."[22] The next week Duncan forwarded "a very handsome and gaily decorated pipe" to Mills. It was a present to Mills from White Bird.[23]

At the same time, however, that this drama unfolded at White Bird's camp, events in Montana were threatening another war between Indians and whites. A small band of Nez Perce returning from Canada were accused of murdering five white men along the way including three white miners on Rock Creek near Philipsburg on July 12, 1878.[24]

According to a white miner who survived the killings on Rock Creek, the Nez Perce knocked on the miners' door and were welcomed into the cabin. The Indians stated they were hungry and the miners started to cook breakfast for them. Then the shooting started, and three of the miners were killed. J. H. Jones, the white survivor, stated, "The Indians when they came into the cabin laughed and talked pleasantly. Some of them could speak very good English. They asked if any of us had been fighting the Nez Perces last summer; whether our ground was paying and many other questions. They said they were good Indians and friendly. The first intimation we had of evil was when they shot Joy."[25]

D. B. Jenkins, a white correspondent from Philipsburg, threatened, "We know no friendly Indians and cannot afford to wait till we are murdered to find out when we meet one whether he is friendly or not. We do not know how to distinguish a Flathead from a Nez Perce or a Crow from a Sioux. But know how and will missionary [kill?] all that come through this valley."[26]

From Rock Creek, the band of Nez Perce hostiles fled through the Bitterroot Valley towards Idaho. In the Bitterroot they were accused of plundering the house of Joe Blodgett, a white settler married to a Salish woman.[27] The Nez Perce were pursued by a United States Army detachment from Fort Missoula led by First Lieutenant Thomas Wallace, and a party of white and Salish Indian volunteers from the Bitterroot Valley. The Salish volunteers pursuing the Nez Perce included Francois Lamoose, Narcisse, Louis Vanderburg, and Martin Charlo.[28]

The troops and white and Salish volunteers tracked the Nez Perce until the trail reached the Idaho border. At the border almost all the volunteers decided to return to their homes, and the troops continued the pursuit accompanied by two or three white civilians. Soon after the troops entered Idaho on July 21, 1878, they caught up with the Nez Perce and attacked them. Six of the Nez Perce were killed, three wounded, and the rest escaped.[29]

The murders and thefts inflamed Montana whites, and many made threats against the Salish Indians who had no part in the depredations. Duncan responded to the situation with "An Appeal to Reason: The Injustice and Folly of Threatening All Indians with Death Because Some Are Murderers."[30] Duncan emphasized his disapproval of the murders committed by the refugee Nez Perce, but he also decried those whites who threatened peaceable Indians in response. He argued,

> Their opinions, however published in a respectable journal...are capable of much greater evils than any individual action, not to mention the absurdity of urging the propriety of killing the first Frenchman met because another had murdered some one — they actually appear to approve of the principle of killing a Frenchman on account of a murder by an Italian. Do they not know that two Indian nations are as separate and distinct as any two nations of Europe? Their customs, languages, modes of living and very often their food and methods of transportation are totally dissimilar. Why a Flathead who last year proved his friendship for, or, if some prefer it, his disinclination to hostility towards the whites, would be subject to be shot by the first white man who has a safe opportunity simply because said white man does not know he is not a hostile Nez Perce passes comprehension.

He also pointed out that random murders of friendly Flathead, Pend d'Oreille, or Spokane Indians would force these tribes to fight the whites. Such an uprising would result in the death of many innocent whites and Indians.[31] Mills published an editorial with Duncan's column maintaining that the threats of Philipsburg whites to kill any Indian on sight were unfortunate but understandable. Mills argued that federal Indian policy prohibited Indians from leaving their reservations without an army escort.[32]

The debate continued and Duncan wrote a column taking issue with Mills' editorial. Duncan pointed out that the right of the Flathead Reservation tribes to hunt buffalo and other game off the reservation was guaranteed by the 1855 Hellgate Treaty. At the time the Philipsburg whites were threatening peaceful Indians, Salish Chief Arlee was returning from a buffalo hunt and could easily have traveled through the Philipsburg area. Duncan could see no reason why the peaceable Salish Indians should be threatened after they "had but lately offered to furnish scouts to warn settlers of any approach of hostiles." White murders of friendly Indians were frequent:

> With reference to your not knowing instances of Indians being killed on account of the misdeeds of their brethren, I will remark that I could cover more space of your valuable sheet than you would be willing to allow with examples thereof....Mr. J. H. Robertson of your place [Deer Lodge] could give you one very glaring case which occurred in Kootenai during his residence there.[33]

In the same issue with Duncan's reply to Mills' editorial, a white correspondent from Philipsburg wrote defending anti-Indian racism and violence: "how many [whites] can look at an Indian and tell his tribe; his face, and tell his intentions? Not one in ten thousand. No one would willingly kill a Flathead for a Nez Perces, but how is one to know?" He then went on with a racist screed that all Indians were dirty thieves: "Who ever saw a really good Indian?"[34] It was against this backdrop of racism and violence, that Duncan's history of the Nez Perce War resumed publication on October 11, 1878.

Duncan took a pack train of flour to the British Columbia Kootenai River country in September 1878. When he reached Tobacco Plains, Duncan found a half dozen lodges of Nez Perce Indians led by Tuk-Alik-Shimsi, a brother of Looking Glass. Tuk-Alik-Shimsi had taken part in the July 1878 council with Lt. Baird at Fort Walsh where Duncan was interpreter.[35]

In November 1878, Duncan headed north with a load of flour he had purchased from the Eddy, Hammond Company in Missoula. On this trip he was headed for Fort Macleod in Alberta. Duncan took Kootenai Chief Eneas and an Indian named Paul as guides. They camped at the foot of a lake on the Middle

Fork of the Flathead River. Duncan carved his name and the date into a large cedar tree near the camp. Soon after, the lake became known as Lake McDonald. Chief Eneas and Paul headed back to the Flathead Reservation while Duncan and the rest of his party continued with the flour. Duncan encountered about twenty lodges of Nez Perce refugees headed back to the United States, but he convinced them that it was too dangerous, and they accompanied Duncan north to Kootenai Lakes. Duncan said he appreciated the help from the Nez Perce as the combined group fought waist deep snow on the way to Kootenai Lakes. The flour was sold to Charles Conrad, the Kalispell area merchant and entrepreneur, who in 1878 had a trading post at Fort Macleod. Duncan returned to Jocko in the spring of 1879.[36]

In January 1879, a controversy broke out over Duncan's account in the *New North-West* of the Nez Perce women and children who were killed at the Battle of the Big Hole. Duncan had written that, "It was shameful the way women and children were shot down in that fight....It is a well known fact that the command wasted more powder and lead on the women and children then on the warriors. There were seventy-eight Indians, all told, killed in the Big Hole battle. Of these, only thirty were warriors. The others were women and children." Duncan charged that the soldiers had murdered forty women and children who had fled and sought shelter in a ravine to get out of the battle.[37]

In an accompanying editorial, Mills argued that some casualties of women and children were unavoidable, but Mills agreed that any deliberate targeting of women and children would be "deserving of censure." Mills wrote that the bodies of the forty women and children in the ravine after the battle had been carried from the camp by the Nez Perce. He understood the Indians had attempted to bury the bodies by caving in the bank to cover them.[38] Duncan wrote Mills a letter, that was not published, maintaining that the women and children in the ravine had been killed there, not in the camp. Mills granted that, if this were true, "we agree with Mr. McDonald that it was cruel and reprehensible in the highest degree."[39]

In early February 1879, two *New North-West* subscribers wrote the newspaper complaining that Duncan's history had failed to mention two Nez Perce-white conflicts just following the Big Hole Battle. Mills forwarded the letters to Duncan for his response.[40]

Duncan wrote on March 21, 1879, that many of the Nez Perce had not known these fights occurred. After special inquiries, Duncan wrote that just after the Big Hole Battle some Nez Perce encountered a party of white men who traded whiskey with them. When fighting broke out, the Nez Perce fired their guns into the pack train of the white men, but they did not know whether any of the white men had been killed.[41]

In Duncan's January 24, 1879, installment of the Nez Perce War history, where he condemned the United States Army for slaughtering women and children at the Big Hole Battle, the *New North-West* made a typesetting mistake. As printed, Duncan said: "The writer of these papers has had many difficulties because he does choose to believe in what the medicine men say." The next week on January 31, 1879, Mills published a correction: "In this his [Duncan's] statement was reversed. It should have read, 'The writer of these papers has had many difficulties because he does *not* choose to believe,' etc."[42]

A few weeks later, Duncan followed up with a personal letter to Mills about Indian religious beliefs which Mills published in the February 21, 1879, issue. Duncan emphasized: "I again repeat my disbelief in Indian medicine. I have said the Indians get vexed with me on account of my unbelief, and although oftentimes placed in embarrassing positions on this account, I remain to this day unconverted." Duncan related his experiences in 1871 or 1873 when he accompanied a Pend d'Oreille war party on the plains that had their horses stolen by the Blackfeet. Duncan joined the Pend d'Oreille who pursued the thieves towards the south fork of the Saskatchewan River. One morning one of the Pend d'Oreille was painted and singing his medicine song. He told Duncan and the rest of the party that unless everyone in the party painted themselves, one of the Pend d'Oreille warriors would lose his life. Duncan objected: "I told the warriors I did not believe the medicine man and would go on no wild goose chase." Finally everyone had painted themselves except Duncan and a person named Linlay. The last two holdouts were forced to join the ceremony, and, according to Duncan's account, "the scene was ludicrous in the extreme."[43]

Duncan felt the traditional medicine beliefs conflicted with the Lord's Prayer and three Hail Mary's the party repeated faithfully three times a day. On the same trip, Pend d'Oreille Chief Michelle used his traditional Indian medicine to call the buffalo for the hunters. Duncan concluded, "Yes, I am a disbeliever, and what intelligent person would not be?"[44]

In March 1879, Mills purchased a "handsome" engraved watch in Helena as a gift for Duncan on completion of the Nez Perce War history.[45] The last installment of Duncan's history appeared in the *New North-West* on March 28, 1879. The last paper described the recent meeting between Nez Perce Chief White Bird and the United States Army representative in July 1878 at Fort Walsh where Duncan was interpreter.[46] The finale was supposed to run on March 14, 1879, but had been delayed in the mail.[47]

Mills noted in the March 14, 1879, issue, "That the publication of these papers has been appreciated is evidenced by the constant demand for back numbers of the *New North-West* containing the history." Since many of the back issues were no longer in print, Mills suggested that "arrangements may possibly be made whereby all those desirous of getting the narrative of the Nez Perces wanderings, as told by Mr. McDonald, will be able to do so." This might have been a suggestion that the history would be published as a book. Mills did note that Duncan had promised to send future "sketches" relating to Indian customs and other topics.[48]

Duncan took a prospecting trip to the Kootenai mines in September 1879 accompanied by Robert McGregor Baird. They spent the winter in Canada. At Tobacco Plains he found the same band of Nez Perce refugees led by Tuk-Alik-Shimsi, who had been

there in September 1878.⁴⁹ In the fall of 1879 the Nez Perce negotiated from Tobacco Plains with Flathead Agent Peter Ronan
to return to the United States. Since they feared the United States
government would send them to exile in Oklahoma with Chief
Joseph's Nez Perce, they decided to remain in Canada.⁵⁰ Duncan
observed, "These Indians are poor but not suffering from starvation. They brought us berries and cooked fish, and meat as gifts,
not expecting anything in return."⁵¹

While at Tobacco Plains, Duncan questioned the Nez
Perce about any white women killed in Idaho during the 1877
war. The Nez Perce said one white woman and a child were killed
accidentally when they hid in the upstairs of a house the Nez
Perce had set on fire. Another white woman and child were killed
by four drunken Nez Perce: "We could have killed many more
women and citizens but our Chief Looking Glass, would not
permit us."⁵² Tuk-Alik-Shimsi and his Nez Perce band moved to
the east side of the Continental Divide because the Kootenay Indians at Tobacco Plains tried to whip the Nez Perce who danced
a traditional Indian dance with Kootenai women.⁵³

According to a letter Duncan sent on October 24, 1879,
Eagle-of-the-Light, the Nez Perce chief who had spent the war at
the Flathead Agency, tried to get White Bird's Nez Perce band to
return to the United States. Sitting Bull refused to allow anyone
to take the Nez Perce from the Sioux camp.⁵⁴

By November 21, 1879, Duncan was at Fort Macleod, and
reported that the Sioux and Nez Perce refugees on the Canadian plains were very hard up for food. Other Nez Perce were at
Kootenai Lakes and living on fish, but Duncan expected them
to commence farming in Canada in the spring. Duncan said he
knew for certain the Nez Perce had not killed any white owned
cattle.⁵⁵

Duncan wrote another letter from Canada from the Kootenai Lakes on December 13, 1879. He was with Tuk-Alik-Shimsi
and ten lodges of Nez Perce Indians. Two hunters killed four
mountain sheep and the next day one of the hunters, three wom-
en, an old man, and a boy started on horseback to get the meat.

The party was caught in a snow storm and the women, old man, and boy could not get off the mountain. Duncan and Tuk-Alik-Shimsi accompanied a rescue party to save those stuck in the snow. Duncan carried the most seriously frozen woman off the mountain on his back.[56]

In the same month of December 1879, Duncan met a band of Mountain Stoney Indians at Kootenai Lakes. The Stoneys were starving and Duncan was able to feed them and give them one hundred pounds of flour. The Stoneys camped with Duncan and the Nez Perce. The Nez Perce were Drummers who followed the Indian prophet Smohalla. They put on a Christmas feast together with talks about their religious beliefs. Duncan sent a summary of the teachings in a report to the *New North-West*.[57]

According to another letter from Canada, Duncan was planning to travel to the plains on February 11, 1880, to interview Sitting Bull and write his life story.[58] By February 29, 1880, however, the snow was so deep that Duncan had to turn back. He had already lost four head of horses. On the plains he met two lodges of Cree Indians who were starving. During fall 1879, he had shipped some flour to Fort Macleod, but he could not get there in February 1880.[59] By March 1880, Duncan had made it to Fort Macleod. Much of the social life at the fort revolved around three to five dances a week. At one dance Duncan and his friends tried to politely ask the Indian girls to dance. They were refused. A French mixed blood told Duncan and his friends they needed to drag the girls out on the dance floor, and then they would "dance plenty."[60]

In May 1880, Duncan made an unsuccessful attempt to return to Montana from the Kootenai Lakes, but he had to retreat north because the snow was too deep.[61] It must have been nearly summer 1880 by the time Duncan returned to Jocko and ended his northern adventure.

The Nez Perces:
The History of Their Troubles and the Campaign of 1877

by Duncan McDonald

It will be remembered that in the year 1847, Dr. [Marcus] Whitman and wife were murdered [by] a Kyuse Indian named Ta-ma-has, who was supposed to have been influenced to commit this by a Mexican named Jo. This murder resulted in a conflict between the U. S. Government and the above named tribe. After the Indians were defeated the Government demanded the murderers, and Ta-ma-has and several others were hung in Willamette Valley, Oregon. At the time the Kyuses were engaged in this war, a young man of the Nez Perce nation named Yellow Bull abandoned his parents and tribe. Ta-ma-has had a young and beautiful daughter, loved and respected by all who knew her. Yellow Bull, by his coolness and personal bravery had won her affections and the confidence of her father, and it was soon agreed upon that the two should wed each other.

After Ta-ma-has was hung the young couple came back to the Nez Perces country, and shortly after the girl gave birth to a son. Little worthy of note transpired regarding this couple until the boy reached the age of manhood. One day, whilst conversing with his mother, he asked her if he ever had a grand-father, and, if so, he would like very much to pay him a visit. Hesitating for a few moments, the woman told him that he had a grand-father, and that he was dead, he having been hung by the Americans a long time ago. This same young man was one of the three who committed the depredations in Idaho last summer.

Later on, in the year 1854, the Nez Perces, then under
Chiefs Lawyer and We-we-tzin-mae, concluded a treaty with the
United States Government. Shortly after this treaty was formed
several Indians and their women were murdered by the whites,
probably without just cause, as we shall endeavor to show. We
refer to one instance in particular, where three Indians started
out to the mountains in search of game. After arriving where
game was plentiful, they had little or no difficulty in procuring a
reasonable supply, and, after caching it returned to their homes,
making an agreement before starting to return at a certain time
and take it home. This being agreed upon the three separated,
and upon their return two met at the cache about the same time.
Feeling somewhat fatigued by their trip, they dismounted to take
a short rest, when two white men approached them in a rude
manner, disarmed them, and asked one of the Indians whether or
not he was the man that interpreted for Chief Joseph. The man
answered him to the contrary. Thompson, the white man, called
him a liar, at the same time knocking the Indian down and abus-
ing him in a brutal manner. The Indian's companion made no
resistance or attempt to save him, but the third one of the party
referred to, named Willatiah, arrived while the scuffle was going
on, and made inquiries as to the cause of it. On being informed
that the Indian had been thus treated without any cause or prov-
ocation whatever, Willatiah at once interfered in hopes to stop
the white man from offering any further abuse, when suddenly
the white man sprang upon him. But Willatiah being a man of
considerable nerve and strength, soon had the white man upon
the ground, when the latter called to his companion to shoot the
— —. The companion obeyed this command — Witlatiah fell a
corpse. The white man who committed this rash act was one of
the squatters of Wallowa valley, and it was supposed a little difficulty he had had with Chief Joseph a short time before was what
prompted him to do the deed. It seems Chief Joseph had ordered
him to quit Wallowa, as he himself claimed that section of country, and requested him to ask Lawyer to give him land, as that he,
Lawyer, had sold his country for molasses sugar to the Govern-

ment. As soon as Wiltatiah expired the remaining two Nez Perces started off quite panic stricken. A short time afterward another Indian reached the scene of the late conflict and found his dead friend and companion, and immediately set out to ascertain the cause. Satisfying himself, he informed Chief Joseph, who at once summoned his warriors and started to interview Agent [John] Montieth, demanding at the same time the murderers.

This request the Agent refused to comply with, only trying to satisfy them by telling them that they ought to kill the white men.

The Nez Perces, Continued.

Wal-litze was the man who fired the first shot in the late Nez Perces war. He was the son of a well-to-do farmer named Tip-piala-natzit-kan, who is a brother of the once favorite Eagle of the Light, and who was murdered by a white man four years ago. Tip-piala-natzit-kan was well known throughout the tribe, and his duty it was to call the councils together. As was mentioned before, the father of Wat-litze was a farmer, and in good circumstances, peaceably inclined towards all, accommodating and undoubtedly desired the settlement of the country in which he lived. About a year prior to the murder of Tip-piala-natzit-kan a white man came to his house and stated that he would like to take up a piece of land, and requested of him to show him a piece of land unclaimed by anyone, promising him (the Indian) to be a good neighbor. Tip-piala-nitzit-kan, liking the appearance of the man, at once granted his request and proceeded to show him the unclaimed land. No difficulty arose between the white man and the Indian until about a year afterward, when the white man wanted to fence a piece of land that the Indian claimed. It seems that early one morning the man was engaged in hauling some rails, a short distance from the Indian's house, when the wife of the Indian roused him up and told him that his white friend was putting some rails upon their land. Tip-piala-nitzit-kan at once aroused the other Indians who were living in his house, and asked them to accompany him, as he wished to talk with the white man and find out what were his intentions, and said that he was afraid to visit him alone. But it seems that no one wanted to accompany him and accordingly he went alone. Upon reaching the designated place he asked the white man if he had forgotten the promise he made to him during their first interview, and asked him in a friendly manner not to put any rails on his land, but put them on the land that he was owner of. The white man at once became wrathy, and taking his rifle from off the pile of rails shot the Indian, wounding him mortally. The Indian at once started for home, suffering great pain, and much exhausted from the loss of blood. His son Wal-litze, was then in the Kiyuse country. The wounded man addressed his people in the following words. "I know that my days are short upon this earth, and it is my desire that you do not get excited at this event, and send this message to my son Wal-litze: Tell him for my sake, and for the sake of his brothers and sisters, and in fact for the whole of the Nez Perces nation, to hold his temper and let not his heart get the best of him. We are as a nation poor in circumstances, in fact we have nothing. The white man has plenty of things that we have not. We can manufacture neither arms nor ammunition. We love our country and above all our families. Do not go to war. You will lose your country by it, and above all the loss of life will be greater. Tell my son I should like to see and shake hands with him before I die, but I am afraid I cannot. When I am dead tell him all I have said and lastly of all not to wage war upon the whites." Saying this he expired a few moments afterward. A few days afterward his son came home, and naturally enough his relatives delivered to him the message left by his dying parent. Wal-litze hung his head as the message was related to him, and with tears running down his cheeks said that he was very sorry to hear of his father being killed in that way and that he felt proud of his last remarks warning himself and people to keep at peace and hold in abhorrence war. Chief Joseph and others demanded the murderer of Tip-piala-natzit-kan, but the authorities refused to take any steps to either arrest or punish him. Joseph then warned the whites that if they did not punish the murderer, there would be trouble. Wal-litze, Tap-sis-ill-pilp, and a young boy whose name is not known, are the three who commenced the depredations in Idaho last summer. Both Wal-litze and Tap-sis-ill-pilp were killed in the battle of Big Hole.

The Nez Perces, Continued.

As further evidence in proof that the attack of the Nez Perces on the White race was not the result of inborn deviltry on the part of the Red man, but rather a continuous abuse and violence exercised by the former on their so-called savage neighbors, I will now give you the history of the murder of a native in the vicinity of Slate Creek, Idaho. Ta-wai-a-wai-we, or Bear Thinker, one of the chiefs of that region, with the accustomed friendliness shown by his people ten years ago toward the whites, received into his family as son-in-law and endowed with a portion of his worldly goods an American whose love of ease o'er leapt his ambition. Unfortunately also for Bear Thinker the mind of his son-in-law was as stagnant as his body, and seemed to have belonged to the Dark Ages when the superstitions of his race were more remarkable than those of the Indians to-day. Among other beliefs indulged in by this worthy was one that his father-in-law being a chief and a Medicine Man, or Wizard, was proof against death otherwise than by old age. This conviction being conveyed to a white acquaintance and backed by a bet, the pair tested the matter by administering to the chief a dose of strych[n]ine, which, it is hardly necessary to add, quickly conveyed him to the happy hunting grounds. Granting that this act originated in an almost incredible ignorance, it appears that a devilish recklessness went hand in hand therewith, as the Indians state that the poisoners enjoyed a hearty laugh while the old man was "kicking his last" and remained wholly unpunished for their crime.

About nine years ago, near Kamiah, a Nez Perces woman was murdered, but I have not been able to gather any particulars, and I have also been informed of the killing of Ta-akill-see-waits, son of a chief of the same name. Of his death nothing is known except that he started on a short trip with a white friend from which he did not return. Sometime after, however, some Indians engaged in hunting discovered traces of blood which being followed led them to the bank of a small creek, where they found the remains of their friend covered with earth and brush. Their applications for the arrest of these and other of their assailants and murderers were of no avail, meeting always with the response that the punishment of a white man would instigate a war, and as yet they were not sufficiently desperate to accept such an issue.

The Nez Perces, Continued.

Before continuing the main subject matter of these papers, permit me shortly to notice an article in the Benton *Herald* in which it is stated that the present writer "will, no doubt, give only the Nez Perces view of the subject, but that is more likely to prove a correct version, [of the troubles and adventures of the tribe than were the reports of the army officers who were outgeneraled by Chief Joseph]."

Now while I deny having the slightest sympathy with murderers or ruffians of any description, whether white or red, I claim the admitted fact that there are generally two sides to a question and one side of the difficulty with the Nez Perces being pretty well understood, I have been prevailed upon to give, to the best of my ability the other, or, Indian version. And both being provided it is more likely that a method of evading such difficulties may more readily be arrived at. Should my humble contributions happen, in any degree, to procure such a desideratum, I shall be more than repaid for any trouble I have taken in gathering data. While thanking the editor of the *Record* for the latter portion of his remarks, I would add that while endeavoring not only to keep within the limits of strict truth, but also to eliminate exaggeration, any obscurity in description of incidents must be met with some allowance of an ignorance on the part of the Indians with regard to dates, and also, in some instances, of civilized names of localities render impossible a more definite writing.

Having so far diverged, I will now continue an account of those actions, which drove the tribe on their path to vengeance.

Chief Joseph

Source: Library of Congress, Photograph Division, Washington, D.C., USZ 62-49148.

On their annual trip to the plains, about the year '64, the
Nez Perces, having dug what camas they required at Big Hole,
proceeded down the Missouri and camped at the junction of a
stream which heads in the Rocky Mountains, southeast of Deer
Lodge. While at that place it seems that a party of Flatheads, under Stalassna, which had been on an unsuccessful horse-stealing
expedition to the Snake country, arrived within a short distance
of the camp. Upon discovering it, however, instead of making
themselves known, they cached themselves till night, when they
stole four fine horses and also stole themselves away. On the following day while the Nez Perces were moving camp they were
overtaken by four well-armed white men who accused them of
stealing horses from the vicinity of Virginia City. Their denial
was, of course, received with utter disbelief, because the whites
had tracked their horses almost into the camp — in fact to the
stopping-place of the Flatheads who were the true thieves — and,
as was natural, although the Nez Perces declared that there must
be some mistake and they themselves had had horses stolen, their
assertions still met with no credence. The white men accordingly
followed the camp until it reached the neighborhood of Bozeman, when, emboldened by the proximity of the settlements,
they shot two Indians, names respectively Ta-wis-wy and Hym-
py-ya-se-ni, who had gone there to trade. The former was killed
at once, but the latter escaped and recovered, although a bullet
entered at the base of the nose and made its exit at the back of
his neck.

At the same period also the whites, determined on a supposed revenge, caught and killed another Indian who was hunting
about eight miles from Bozeman. These acts were more than Indian nature could be expected to submit to and accordingly the
Indians determined on an assault on the settlements. Such an
unfortunate occurrence, was, however, at that time avoided by
the intervention of a Delaware named John Hill, who, acting as
interpreter between the races, procured the holding of a common
council, in which the Nez Perces were promised that the murderers should be arrested, taken to Virginia [City] and made to

undergo a lawful punishment for their acts. Of course the promise was a dead letter. Equally of course, no one who has followed the published accounts of the Nez Perces war will argue that the then peaceful result of the conference was due to cowardice on the part of the Indians.

Reckless as the actions of the above mentioned whites really were, there are yet many men in the west who would sympathize therewith and with some show of reason, as the former certainly had strong cause for belief that the Nez Perces had stolen their horses; but who can excuse the killing of U-mas-na-cow and Key-la-tzie-auth (Hand-Otter), two of the tribe murdered in the vicinity of Lewiston, in '68 or '69, simply because they attempted to prevent two white men, who had brought whisky into their lodge, from debauching their women. The next murder of my list seems to have been committed merely on account of the belief (shared and stated, according to a late report, by Gen. [Philip] Sheridan) that only a dead Indian can be a good one. The circumstances connected therewith being as follows: In 1871 my informant had his lodge pitched on the present site of the Missoula post, when two Nez Perces arrived thereat on the way from the main camp, then on the Gallatin, to their homes in Idaho. During the night of their stay with him, another Nez Perce *en route* from Idaho also made his appearance, and in giving the home news told one of the others that his wife was anxiously awaiting his return. This much pleased the Indian addressed, for in some manner he had been led to believe that, during his winter's hunt on the plains the woman had allowed proximity to have the stronger charms, and replaced him with another husband. Such a story having been circulated in the camp and the forsaken husband — so understood — being a man of mark he had been offered as second wife a young girl, one of the most eligible of the tribe. Being, however, of a constant disposition, before stating his acceptance he determined to more accurately inquire as to his wife's faithlessness. For this reason he had started for home ahead of the camp, leaving therewith his baggage, and extra animals. Upon hearing the news as above

stated he concluded to return to the camp for his belongings so as
not to arrive at home empty handed. He therefore left the Bitter
Root and was on the road within twenty or twenty-five miles
of Bozeman when a man stepped out of a roadside house and
without speech of any description shot him through the body.
By catching the saddle he managed to remain on his horse until
he was carried some distance from the scene of the attack. He
then fell to the ground when he crawled sufficiently to be out
of sight of white passers and thus he remained for two days and
nights without food or water, when at last some Indians came
along they bore him to the camp a few miles on the other side of
Bozeman. Soon after his arrival thereat some soldiers appeared
with an order for the camp to move, the order having originated
on account of some depredations committed in the vicinity by
other Indians — Sioux or Crows. All the Nez Perces then — with
the exception of Eagle of the Light who had a dying brother in
his lodge and preferred to take the responsibility of staying to
either leaving his brother or killing him by travel — left for the
Yellowstone, and on their way the wounded man died.

An Indian more or less is truly no great matter, but surely
a great country which can afford to free her negroes, and boasts
of her Bergh may also exhibit a slight feeling of humanity for the
family ties of a poor Red Man.

The Nez Perces, Continued.

Many more cases of outrage committed against the Nez
Perces as individuals could be added to the foregoing, but a sur-
feit, perhaps, having already been given it is now apropos, shortly,
to call attention to the great cause of dissatisfaction on the part of
that tribe. The Stevens' Treaty of 1855, under which the Government claims the control of those Indians, was obtained by a ruse,
which, if understood, could hardly receive the commendation of
a great nation. Not being able to gain to his aim the consent of
any of the real chiefs, Governor [Isaac I.] Stevens, a man of much
ability and few scruples, cut the Gordian knot for the Govern-

ment by providing a chief freshly manufactured for the occasion. Lawyer, recognized by the Indians as a tobacco cutter (a sort of under secretary) for the chiefs Looking Glass, Eagle-of-the-Light, Joseph and Red Owl, was the chosen man. In other words, for certain considerations he was prevailed upon to sign away the rights of his brethren — rights over which he had not the slightest authority — and, although he was a man of no influence with his tribe, the Government, as in duty bound on account of his great services, conferred upon him the title and granted him the emoluments of Head Chief of the Nez Perces. The feelings of the Indians were at that time aroused to such a pitch of indignation that they at first determined to hang their new superior, but, as with them, so often has been the case, milder counsels prevailed, and indifference and contempt took the place of revenge. Of course, as will be supposed — however the Government chose to look upon the result — the true chiefs and body of the people regarded the treaty as void, and thus the case stood — gradual encroachments being made on one side and protests being made by the other, until last year when the old story of a love affair produced the grand *denouement.*

Before, however, proceeding with a description of attendant circumstances thereof, I will, to prevent misconception, give a short resume regarding the chiefs connected with the council held during the formation of the aforesaid treaty. As previously hinted, there were at that time four noted chiefs and these were: 1st. Eagle-of-the-Light, Chief of the Took-peh-mas and Lum-ta-mas, first among his peers as to eloquence, and chosen by them as main spokesman at the council. Partly on account of old age and partly due to a conviction arrived at through an intelligent intercourse with white men, that his people had no chance of redressing their wrongs by fighting, he declined to take part in the late war, and has since its commencement chiefly resided in Montana.

2d. Flint Color, or, as better known by Americans, Looking Glass, a chief of the Took-peh-mas, and perhaps the most influential man of the nation. He was father of the late Looking

Chief Looking Glass

Source: National Anthropological Archives, Smithsonian Institution
Washington, D.C., inv. 01005001, photo lot 4420,
photo by William Henry Jackson, 1871.

Glass, (known to the Flatheads as Big Hawk), who was killed in the battle with General Miles north of Fort Benton.

3d. Joseph, Chief of the Ca-moo-ey-nahs, father of the present well-known leader. Before death he cautioned his son against giving white men any opportunity to claim his land. "The Wallowa valley," said he, "is yours. It is a fine country and belonged to your fathers, who are buried here. It will yield a subsistence for you and yours. Let the white man travel through it, and, while doing so, eat your fish and partake of your meat, but receive from him no goods or other presents or he will assert that he has purchased your country."

And 4th. Red Owl, another chief of the Took-peh-mas, an eloquent, sagatious [sic] Indian, noted as an Apollo among belles of the tribe. He was wounded during the attack made by Miles, but whether fatally or not I have been unable to learn.

It may be here added that at the period now spoken of White Bird, latterly of so much notoriety, was young and of no particular prominence. Since then, however, he gradually rose in the estimation of his associates, and on the resignation of Eagle-of-the-Light, became the first chief of the Lum-ta-mas.

The Nez Perces Campaign, Continued.
The Council of the Nez Perces and Crows and How the Former Were Deceived.

After telling how three men, Walitze, Tip-sis-ill-pilp, and U-em-till-lip-cown, murdered the settlers of Camas Prairie, we will endeavor to explain more about them. It was known that Walitze was a son of Tipia-la-na-tzi-kan, a councillor [sic] who was murdered near his field on account of a quarrel about rails. Tip-sis-ill-pilp was a grandson of the Cayuse Indian, Tam-a-hus, who murdered Dr. [Marcus] Whitman and wife in 1847. U-em-till-lip-cown was a grandson of Tipia-la-na-tzi-kan, a brother of the well known chief, Eagle-of-the-Light.

It seems that the Nez Perces and the Crows were greatest of friends once. They used to camp together and kill buffalo every winter for many years. The "Women Nation," the Crows, is what the Nez Perces call them since the Nez Perces campaign against the United States government in 1877. The Crows are named women and some times traitors. It will be explained how they were named. It seems the Nez Perces were influenced by the Crows and urged in a good many respects. The main blame lies on the shoulders of the Crow nation. It is true a man has no right to murder when he is told to do so by another party; but ignorance commits the crime sometimes. Ignorance makes the Indian think all white men are thieves and nothing else, and sometimes they think they can whip the United States government and they really think that there are no good, honest white men. We know that many an Indian has been made chief not for his shrewdness but for his bravery. Any brave Indian can be made a chief. If he were really an idiot, as long as he is brave, his valor covers a multitude of sins. But it is not often the case with wise Indians. It is a hard matter for a wise Indian to become a chief, but any stupid brave can be one with very little opposition.

No doubt the well known Crow chief, named The-Eagle-that-Shakes-Himself was a brave man, but he was not a man of knowledge. Many a day and night the Crow chiefs and Nez Perces spent their time counciling in their lodges about the pale-faced white men. We remember about it. For three years before the war broke out in 1877 between the U.S. Government and the Nez Perces it was told around our campfires what the Crow tribe were trying to do to make an agreement between the two mentioned tribes. We will state an incident that took place about two years ago between the Nez Perces and Crow nations.

We know it to be a fact that when The-Eagle-that-Shakes-Himself once spoke and told Looking Glass and White Bird about the time when the two Nez Perces were murdered by white men, one of them near Bozeman and the other near the Missouri River, exclaimed this chief: "I understand. You are chiefs. Listen to me. I want to let you know how my heart feels towards the white man. Do you see my eyes are open? As long as I live these eyes are open. Never will I allow a white man to take or kill any of my people. You are cowards. You have not the heart that I have.

You are a lot of cowards and like to eat the white man's sugar and molasses. You allow them to take your people's lives. You allow them to spill your own blood on your own soil because they don't tell the truth to the Red Man. I say, fight them. Take their murderers and kill them. What are they good for only to murder the Indians and take our country away? You will get all the help from me. Let us go to war against the white man. You go back to your country and start in, and as soon as I get the news I shall do the same thing. At the same time move this way and I will go to Sitting Bull and make peace with him and we will all give the white man a game." Unfortunately this chief was made a game of by Sitting Bull's warriors. He was killed by the Sioux Indians in a fight between the Sioux tribe and the Crows.

This kind of advice from the Crows had quite an effect on the Nez Perces tribe, especially among the young braves. It was repeated over and over. But Looking Glass never was made a fool of; never was fool enough to take such advice from any of his Indian friends. Looking Glass, after the Crow chief had made his speech, raised his head and resting his eyes on The-Eagle-that-Shakes-Himself, as though they would pierce him, said to the Crow chief: "You say you have eyes. You say you can see. You can flatter a fool, but not me. Those eyes of yours and your heart do not see far. You are like a child; you can see, but cannot see far ahead. You are the men who are fond of sugar and molasses. You are the men who suckle the white man. You are the men that can be bought and sold for a plug of tobacco. I, Looking Glass, Eagle-of-Light and Joseph's father, were the ones who wanted to hang Lawyer for signing treaties with Governor Stevens. What right had he, or authority, to sign treaties? He does not belong to the blood. He is the offspring of a foreigner. We blame him in signing the treaty. But he was not half as bad as Stevens. What right has Stevens to put Lawyer at the head of a nation that really does not belong to him? Is it right for any Indian to go to whoever the head man of the United States may be and put him out of his office and have any one he pleases succeed him? Will the people of the United States like it? No. The Indian that would put the President out of his office would be killed at once. This is what Governor Stevens did with our Indians. We don't want any treaties. Whoever made this world never told the Red Man to sell his country. For this reason, we want to live in peace. If we sign treaties and then turn and fight the Government, it would be breaking up treaties. We do not want to fight as long as we have justice. That is all we want. If the white man punishes his murderers, we shall do the same. But he does not. He does not even ask us to help him. The first thing he calls on is his weapons to kill the Indians. I want peace with the white man. My hand is open to the white man. I do not know what they mean. Whenever one of my Indians gets killed, they do not even arrest the perpetrators. By the looks of things, we will be compelled to go to war."

These Indians, on reaching Idaho from their Buffalo stamping ground, learned that Willatiah was innocently murdered in the mountains by two white men. This Indian's life was really a cause of many a poor innocent settler losing his life in Idaho. Willatiah was the last man murdered before the war broke out in 1877.

The Nez Perces War of 1877, Continued.
The Causes and Councils Leading To It.

I give below a list of Nez Perces Indians killed by whites before the war of 1877.

The Alleged Provocation

Chief Bear-Thinker was poisoned; Juliah was killed near Bozeman without cause; Taivisyact was shot while passing on horseback a house near the Missouri river on the road to Bozeman; Took-kay-lay-yoot, Lapwai, by a soldier on account of liquor; Yalmay-whotzoot, Lapwai, was killed while looking for horses; Him-p-augh, was killed on account of buying a pistol; Tip-iala-huana-chino-mouch at Elk City, cause unknown; Koyotes, was killed on a spree with supposed friends at Slate creek; Maltze-qui was killed because he was falsely accused of stealing a bottle of whisky; Eya-makoot, a woman, was killed with a pick on account of her dog whipping a white man's dog; Cass-say-u was accidentally killed by the son of their own minister, [Henry H.] Spaulding, who shot at another Indian while gambling, and killed the wrong man. Took-ooghp-ya-mool on Salmon River; Usay-kay-act was taken away by a white friend and never seen again; T-nan-na-say a Councilman, was shot by a soldier in a council south of Yakima; Tipia-la-natzi-kan because his field was taken from him; Willatiah in the mountains near Wallowa.

The Threat of War

As I have stated before, none of the murderers of these people were ever arrested or punished. At the time of this last occurrence Joseph and his band were so excited at seeing the murderer of Willatiah go at large that they threatened the settlers of Idaho. The settlers frightened by these threats sent a dispatch to the soldiers at Walla Walla. When the soldiers arrived the officer in command asked Joseph if he wished to fight the whites. Joseph answered, "If I am compelled I will have to fight. The man we wanted to fight for is dead and gone. It is better to be at peace once more. But I warn the whites to not kill any more of my Indians. I would not mind if you were killing Indians who are trying to do something wrong, but it seems you want to kill my best men, and for this cause I will not stand any more murder. I did not ask you to come and settle in my country. If you do not like us keep away."

Councilling [sic] with [Gen. O. O.] Howard

It was then the Nez Perces first heard there was a Big Chief of the soldiers coming to see the Nez Perces nation. They were told this by the soldiers, and the Big Chief coming was Howard. This was in 1876. It should be remembered that there are two brothers, each named Joseph. Joseph, Senior, is the one now a prisoner at Leavenworth. On hearing of this appointed council, Wa-lame-moot-key, a Kayuse chief and a relative of the Josephs, sent for all the Nez Perces chiefs saying he wished to have a council with them near Walla Walla. But the chiefs were not disposed to have a council and remained at home.

But Joseph, Jr., who had heard from other sources that Howard was at Walla Walla, took four or five other Indians and went there to see him.

Howard met him and said, "Joseph, I am glad to see you. But you have come alone; I would like to see the other chiefs also, and to-morrow I will see you." Howard told them to find lodgings in some of the houses of the town and ordered that they should have something to eat. Joseph declined to be quartered off on the town or to accept government board, and did not remain in town.

Next morning they were called to the military post by Howard, and entered the room where he was. Before taking their seats General Howard said to Joseph that "the Sioux chief Spotted Tail had concluded to move to a new reservation."

Joseph merely replied, "and so Spotted Tail finally concluded to remove."

While Joseph was being seated Howard drew some papers from his pocket and said to him: "These papers are my instructions from the Great Father to move all Indians to the reservation. I want to move the Indians to three different reserves. These Indians must go either across the Columbia, to Lapwai or Kamiah reserves." Joseph made no reply. Howard drew out more papers and said, "Joseph, do you understand? All Nez Perces Indians must move to their reserve. Have you anything to say?"

Joseph replied, "Yes, I have. Howard, you are a chief and I am a chief. You know what is good for your white friends and I know what is good for my people. I think it is better to leave all the Indians alone and to leave all the whites alone. I always feel happy in seeing both living in peace. Both peoples are getting civilized and making progress in this part of the country. Both are growing wealthy. When the whites first came here they were poor and we helped them by trading. We gave them everything they wanted. All these things I tell you come from the root of my heart. It is impossible to order all white men to leave; I think it is impossible for all Indians to leave. As I said before the white

General Otis O. Howard

Source: Library of Congress, Photograph Division, Washington, D.C., USZ 62-52494.

man helps the Indian to become civilized and the Indian helps the white man to get rich."

Howard answered, "Yes, Joseph, but you must move."

Joseph again said: "Howard, you had better leave the Indians alone. You are well paid to move Indians from their homes. These Indians are rich and well fixed. I like to see both nations progress. Let the white man raise his children and harvests. The Indian will do the same. We are non-treaty Indians. Therefore we wish to live among the white men and live in peace. It makes me happy when I travel through this fertile country and see that it will support both the Indian and the white man. I have good reason for not wishing to remove to the reserve. It is too small to sustain half my stock. How could we keep our stock on a reserve that is only half large enough to feed it?"

Howard replied, "You must go to the reserve." Joseph said, "Well, you will have to talk with the other chiefs. You are made a chief by your people. You have now a good part of the country. It is better to leave the Indians alone on their own farms. You are working for the White man and I am doing the same for the Red man. We are self-supporting Indians. We ask nothing from the government but protection in our rights."

Howard answered, "Your argument is very good, but I am sorry to say you must go to the reserve." At the same time he told Joseph that he would telegraph to Washington.

Joseph rose and said: "I am telling you how the Indians feel about this country. You say these Indians must go to three different reserves — Lapwai, Kamiah and across the Columbia River. If I must go to a reserve I want to go to the Kayuse reserve and if the Kayuse Indians want to go to Lapwai they can. My Indians can do as they please, but I know they will not go. I do not want a white man to select a place for them. Let the Indians select a place for themselves as white men do. I do not wish the Nez Perces to go to three different reserves. If the Kayuses go to Lapwai I want the whites to leave that part of the country, because it is too small for the Indians alone. We are rich and have many horses and cattle."

Howard replied, "There are too many settlers in the country to be removed on account of the Indians wishes."

Joseph said, "There is the trouble. You say your people are too well settled to be disturbed, and I say the Indians are too well settled to be disturbed. So it is better to leave the Indians alone. Why are you so determined to remove them? This is where we were born and raised. It is our native country. It is impossible for us to leave. We have never sold our country. Here we have all we possess, and here we wish to remain."

Howard merely said: "It is impossible. I wish to have a big talk with all the Indians at Lapwai in ten days' notice."

Joseph then drew out a paper on which were written the words of his father a few moments before he expired. It was as follows:

"My sons, this country is ours. My sons, do not give up this part of the country to the white man."

The paper was handed to Howard who, after reading it, said: "Joseph, you and all the other chiefs come to Lapwai in ten days." It was so agreed.

The Nez Perces War of 1877, Continued.
The Last Council With Howard at Lapwai.

In fulfillment of the wish expressed by Howard to Joseph, Junior, the Nez Perces Chiefs congregated at the Lapwai Agency at the time specified. Joseph, Jr., on reaching home had related to the Nez Perces what Howard had said about their removal, and they were much alarmed. Joseph said to his people that he had done his best to prevent their being removed, and asked them to keep quiet, and so they went to Lapwai. After arriving there, [John] Monteith, the U.S. Indian Agent, told a member of the tribe named Reuben, "You go and see Joseph and tell him to come to the reservation at once. Why are they humbugging and holding councils?" Reuben reported to the Indians what Monteith had said, and it seems had said still more that the Indians "must move." Much anger was created among the Indians at this message. Reuben on seeing Howard afterward told him, "If you are determined to move these peaceful Indians to a place where they cannot graze half their stock, you will have to do it with soldiers. We will always tell you the place is too small."

Howard did get soldiers, and when the Indians saw them reach Lapwai they became more angry than ever. The next question was who the Indians would have for a Speaker at the Council. They held a Council among themselves to select an Indian who was a good talker. The Nez Perces Chiefs were all present except Looking Glass and Red Owl, who were in the mountains hunting, and neither they nor their people had any intimation of what Howard proposed to do with them. The result of the Council was the election for speaker of an Indian named T-whil-who-tzoot, who was supposed to be a smart, intelligent Indian. Joseph, Jr., was barred out, the Council deciding that he was not smart nor bold enough to represent them in a council with Howard.

When the day for the great Council arrived, all the Indians except the two Chiefs mentioned and their people, were present. Joseph, Jr., felt aggrieved at the action of his people in electing another instead of himself as Speaker, withdrew from active participation and the reader will not often see his name mentioned during the campaign. When the council assembled General Howard and the Indians took their seats. The General then arose and said: "I want all these Indians to go to their reserve at once. If you do not go voluntarily, I will compel you to do so with my soldiers. I have instructions from Washington to move all Indians to their reserves and according to my instructions I must make you move. If you will not move for my words, you shall go to the reserve by the points of my soldiers' bayonets."

The elected Chief, or Speaker, T-whil-who-tzoot, rose and said: "Howard, I understand you to say you have instructions from Washington to move all the Nez Perces nation to the reserve. You are always talking about *Washington*. I would like to know who Washington is? Is he a Chief, or a common man, or a house, or a place? Every time you have a council you speak of Washington. Leave Mr. Washington, that is if he is a man, alone.

He has no sense. He does not know anything about our country. He never was here. And you are always talking about your soldiers. What do we care about your fighting qualities? You are chief, Howard, and I am elected by the Nez Perces to speak for them and do the best I can for my people. Let us settle the matter between you and me."

Howard replied, "I have instructions from Washington to move all Indians to the reserves and put them under charge of Agent Monteith."

T-whil-who-tzoot said, "Howard, are you trying to scare me? Are you going to tell me the day on which I shall die? I know I must die some day."

Howard then turned to White Bird and said, "Have you anything to say?"

White Bird answered, "We have elected T-whil-who-tzoot to speak for all the Nez Perces. Whatever he says or does is law with us."

T-whil-who-tzoot was at once arrested and put in the guard house, where he remained about a week. If I have been rightly informed, Howard in that Council came near being a victim at the hands of the Nez Perces warriors.

The Nez Perces War of 1877, Continued.
The Immediate Cause of the Outbreak.

When Howard saw the Indians abandoning him on account of their elected speaker going to jail, he sent for White Bird. When the chief arrived, Howard said to him: "I want you and Joseph and all the rest of the Nez Perces to go to the reservation."

Little Bald Head (or known as The Preacher), said to Howard: "I would like to select a place for my people. The place where I want to live is opposite Lapwai."

"I don't want any Indian to select a place outside of the reserve," said Howard. "I want Joseph, White Bird and all Nez Perces to go where I wanted them to go. If not, as I said before, I shall move the Indians with bullets or bayonets. I only give you ten days to move to the reserve. If you do not do what I have said

I shall send my soldiers and drive all your stock to the reserve, and also the Indians, and disarm them."

White Bird replied: "We like our country; we are wealthy Indians and self-supporting; we do not wish the government to spend a dollar toward the Nez Perces; my white neighbors are my friends."

Then and there Joseph, Sr., spoke to Howard: "You give us ten days to move our live stock and property. You must be joking. I notice when you want to move it takes a long time to do it, especially when there are rivers to cross. I notice whenever you go after Indians in time of war it takes you months to cross a river. I want you to understand that we have more horses than the soldiers ever had in the Indian wars: we want time. Ten days is no time for us. When the generals have a handful of soldiers and a few animals to cross a river, it takes them weeks and months to cross. We have plenty of children, women, horses and cattle, and the rivers are high." This is the only speech Joseph, Sr., ever made during the year of 1877.

Howard said again, "I don't want any hum-bugging. Do as I tell you to do — move immediately to the reserve."

Joseph said, "We like hunting; why should we stop on the reserve all the time for the balance of our days?"

Howard: "If you want to hunt you have to get a permit from the United States Indian Agent. Whenever you want to hunt do not take many horses; take as few as possible then you will not bother the settlers. Those settlers are the ones who sent a petition to Washington to get all Indians removed."

All this time Wallitz, Tap-sis-ill-pilp and U-em-till-lilp-cown were listening to what Howard and their chiefs had said. Howard told the chiefs, "You can have any houses on the reserve belonging to the whites and the white men will leave their homes and go to some other places. Those houses are on the reserve, if you wish to occupy those houses all right, and those white men can take your places outside of the reserve — a kind of an exchange."

On these conditions, Joseph, Sr., White Bird and Little Baldhead, or the Preacher, started out with the General to select homes for themselves. While riding around the country Howard had a few soldiers and an interpreter along with him. Howard said to White Bird, "What made you a chief? I am a chief because I lost my arm while fighting in big battles and fought bravely." Joseph and White Bird were surprised at these remarks and said amongst themselves "Howard is anxious for war."

All this time there was news amongst the Indians that the soldiers were increasing at Lapwai or some place near.

The Indians were advised by their white friends they would be compelled to move; that Howard was determined to move all Indians. Young Joseph on hearing that there were plenty of soldiers arriving near them exclaimed: "I see that Howard is determined to move Indians and stock. If Howard tries to move my stock or trouble me I shall fight him at once."

When the Indians saw Howard's actions they thought they were bound to fight. Then the Indians concentrated at Camas Prairie to have councils and decide how they should act and what was the best thing for them to do. While camped at Camas Prairie councilling [sic], the three murderers made up their minds what to do.

We explained before that Walitz was insulted at this time. Looking Glass and Red Owl were camped in another place near Clearwater by themselves. Again and again the Indians were told by their white friends, "You must go; if not you will be compelled to fight Howard." At the same time the three murderers were told "the settlers at Camas Prairie were the ones who sent a petition to Washington to get the Indians removed." Looking Glass on hearing that the soldiers and Indians were at the point of war, sent his brother, Took-alix-see-ma, who is now with Sitting Bull, to tell Joseph and White Bird "not to fight." Took-alix-see-ma went from Looking Glass' camp three different times. He was sent by his brother to do the best he could to keep the Indians in peace. He was an influential man.

The murderers on learning the parties that were trying to get the Indians removed said: "Well, there is nothing dearer than our country and our lives. I, Walitz, was insulted on account of a girl I took for a wife. Now, my friends, let us go and buy arms from the settlers. Some of our friends tell us to buy arms and be prepared for Howard. We might as well start in. Let us kill the parties around Camas Prairie, because they are the ones that sent the petition to Washington. We must make them leave our dear soil before we do. It was bad enough to kill our fathers and they get no punishment, and now they, not satisfied by getting the greatest part of our country and arresting our speaker, must send a petition to Washington to get soldiers to take our country that is dear to us. Let us all die and let somebody else get our country."

While having councils at Camas Prairie, Joseph, Sr., was preparing to go to the buffalo country. The two brothers Joseph started from Camas back towards Wallowa valley to kill some cattle and dry some meat. Took-alex-see-ma was running around detailed by his brother Looking Glass to keep the Indians quiet. As Took-alex-see-ma told us once in his tent: "When I reached White Bird's camp the third time my brother sent me, we were in a large lodge and eating dinner, and while I was delivering the message that my brothers sent to the other chiefs, I heard an Indian making a speech on horseback. I recognized him as Big-of-the-light, mounted on a black horse and a gun in his hand, saying, "What are you councilling [sic] about? War is commenced. This black horse I am riding is a white man's horse. This gun is a white man's gun, &c. Wallitze, Tap-sis-ill-pilp, U-em-till-lilp-cown just got back. They murdered four white men and they brought this horse, gun, saddle, &c." At the same time Joseph nor Looking Glass were in camp. White Bird was the only chief there.

Insulting Wallitze by other Indians and Howard arresting their speaker was their reason for starting out to murder, besides Howard's actions toward them were rather mean telling them he would move them with bullets or bayonets.

The Nez Perces War of 1877, Continued.
White Bird Rallies His Band

When the tidings that the three Indians mentioned had murdered four white men the night previous reached White Bird's camp, that chief said:

"Now, my people, we must do the best we can. It is a great crime to murder white men, especially innocent ones. In time of peace you have no right to kill people, either by night or day. If we are forced to go to war then you can do as you please, except that you must not kill women. Neither I nor Joseph told you to kill these men."

The Josephs Sent For

As stated before both the Josephs were absent at the time of the murder of these four men. It seems, however, a messenger went speedily across the Salmon River and towards Wallowa Valley searching for the Josephs, to tell them the news of the murders committed on Camas Prairie. The two brothers were met by the messenger and were told of the crimes committed by Wallitze, Tap-sis-ill-pilp and Um-till-lill-cown. As soon as the brothers Joseph learned the news they dismounted, cut the ropes by which the loaded meat was lashed to their pack animals, and proceeded with all speed to White Bird's camp. On reaching it Joseph and White Bird ordered camp to be moved toward the camp of Looking Glass and Red Owl, but before reaching it these latter chiefs had heard from Took-alix-see-na, a brother of Looking Glass, of the crimes committed by White Bird's band. Before reaching the camp of Looking Glass the three murderers again started out in the dead of night and murdered five or six more men.

Looking Glass Declares for Peace

Anger is an insufficient expression to convey the feeling of Looking Glass when be saw White Bird's camp moving toward him. He said to Joseph and White Bird: "My hands are clean of white men's blood, and I want you to know they shall so remain. You have acted like fools in murdering white men. I will have no part in these things, and have nothing to do with such men. If you are determined to fight go and fight yourselves and do not

attempt to embroil me or my people. Go back with your warriors; I do not want any of your band in my camp. I wish to live
in peace."

The First Battle of the War

On hearing these words Joseph and White Bird made camp
a few miles from Looking Glass. They made up their minds not
to trouble him because he did not wish to go to war. The next
day they moved towards Salmon river in nearly the same direction from which they had come and camped at a place called
Camas Prairie. Early in the morning the camp was alarmed by
one of the Indians. This Indian had been out nearly all night and
about dawn of day the saw some soldiers approaching the camp.
(Before the fight with these soldiers they attacked some freight
teams on the road and killed two or three men.) White Bird had
only 75 warriors in the camp, but they rallied and started out to

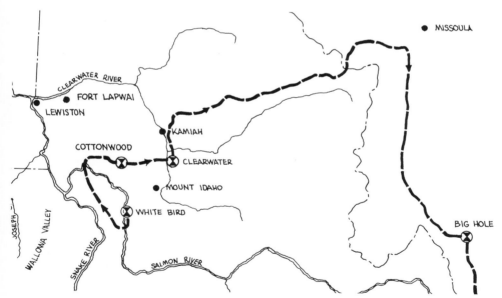

Route of the Nez Perce
Source: John D. McDermott, *Forlorn Hope: The Battle of White Bird Canyon
and the Beginning of the Nez Perce War* (Boise: Idaho State Historical Society,
1978), p. 130

meet the soldiers coming and ascertain what they wanted. But before White Bird had a chance to speak the soldiers opened fire on the Nez Perces. Then the fight opened and there they fought I know not how many hours, but in a short time they surrounded the troops and the Indians charged upon them. White Bird urged his warriors on, saying: "Now is your time to fight. We are attacked. You have been looking for a fight with the white men and now you have got it. Fight now to the last. I want my warriors shot in the breast, not in the back."

They defeated the troops in a short time and killed 35 of them. Of the Indians not one was killed and only four wounded. It is said by some that Joseph was away at the time of this fight. The Nez Perces did not move camp that day. This was the first battle of the campaign and occurred near Salmon river.

The Nez Perces War of 1877, Continued.
Joseph and White Bird in Doubt

The day succeeding the defeat of the soldiers White Bird did not move camp, but the next he moved and crossed the Salmon River the same day. Here he went into camp and remained about four days. Their next move was in a southwesterly direction through Joseph's country — that is, Wallowa valley — and camped in the mountains. Joseph and White Bird ordered camp to move at daybreak the next morning, and they moved back to and across the Salmon river again. The following day they moved again and reached a large plain where there are some pine trees. Here they camped again.

All this time they were councilling [sic] to determine what was best to do — whether they should leave the region of country which they were in and move toward the Snake country, or go to the Buffalo Plains and join Sitting Bull in the British Possessions. Some wanted to surrender to Howard, but they feared they would be shot or hung.

Looking Glass Desired Peace

All this time Red Owl and Looking Glass were camped on a tributary of Clearwater. Looking Glass believed be was safe from assault, believing be had done that which would commend him to the whites by rejecting the proposals of Joseph and White Bird to go to war, and sending them peremptorily away from his camp.

He even saved the life of a white man who was captured and who happened to be a friend of theirs. Looking Glass told his warriors not to molest the man, as he did not wish to see any war between the whites and Indians. At this time he knew a force of soldiers were moving toward his camp. He said to the white man: "Go and tell the whites that I, Looking Glass, am not with the hostiles. I do not wish to fight, and will not unless I am compelled to in self-defense. I saved your life because I am a friend of the whites. I do not wish to be regarded or treated as a hostile. [I] even quarrelled [sic] with my relatives who were coming to my camp because they were hostiles. Now, my friend, go and meet the soldiers. Tell them I am camped at this place and wish very much to see the officer in command. I do not want any trouble."

The man started with the message, but instead of meeting it he avoided the command and returned to the camp. He told the chief the soldiers were coming and not far off, and he believed they would attack the camp. Looking Glass ordered some of his men to go and see how far away the soldiers were. This was early in the morning. Two or three of the Indians started in the direction the soldiers were coming, but just as the soldiers reached the bank of the creek the soldiers charged on the camp.

The Attack on Looking Glass' Camp

When the chief saw the soldiers coming he started toward them with the white man he had tried to send as a messenger. Looking Glass made signs to the soldiers to halt, that he wished to speak to them, but his signs had no effect. Almost immediately the bullets were flying thick. The white man got away from the chief and ran to the soldiers. Looking Glass returned to his camp and told his men to do the best they could. He then had about eleven lodges. The Nez Perces fled in all directions. One woman who tried to swim across the stream with her child in her arms had gotten about half way across when she was shot and was drowned. The soldiers captured about 1200 head of horses. The most of these animals belonged to the two chiefs. The soldiers burnt everything Looking Glass had in his camp.

Talk about savages being blood-thirsty fiends! If these soldiers were not blood-thirsty fiends, then there is no savage in this world. Even had it been Joseph or White Bird who endeavored to have a talk with the commanding officer of the opposing force, they were entitled to it. There is no law of civilized war that gives a right to shoot a man when he is trying to surrender. Neither Joseph nor White Bird knew of the fight. The soldiers killed no one but the woman who was trying to cross the stream with her child. Is it possible that if a soldier cannot kill a buck Indian that he has a right to shoot at a woman?

The Sad Fate of Mrs. [J. J.] Manuel

Before continuing the narrative succeeding the attack on Looking Glass' camp, I will relate an incident preceding. It seems that at the earliest commencement of the Nez Perces war there were two white women murdered. One of the them was murdered by an Indian who was drunk. The other white woman was burned in a house with her child. When her husband and others were murdered by the Nez Perces she went up stairs. The Indians say they did not see her at the time of killing the men. When the Indians got possession of the house Joseph, Jr., was present. He was sitting at one side of the place smoking his pipe. He was asked by the warriors what should be done — whether they should set fire to the house or leave without destroying it. All this time the woman and child were up stairs, but the Indians say they did not know it. Young Joseph answered: "You have done worse deeds than burning a house. You never asked our chiefs what was best to be done. You have murdered many men and not asked advice of your chiefs. You can do as you please about the house."

Some of the young men lit a match and set fire to the building. They then went back a little and sat down to watch it burn. They were suddenly startled by the piercing screams of a woman in the second story of the house. Young Joseph ordered them to put out the fire. The young Indians ran down to the water, filled their hats, threw it on the flames, and tried every way they knew to extinguish the fire and to save the woman. But it was too late. She and her child perished.

The same young warriors who were with Joseph, Jr., at the time told me that when he left the place Joseph held down his head for a long time, and at last looking up he said they had done very wrong in burning the woman, that he was very sorry; that he had believed the house empty.

The burning of this poor, harmless woman looks very bad for the Indian side. Still there is some blame should attach to the white man. The white man does wrong in allowing the Indian to have whisky. It is easy to reply that the Indians take the whisky away from them by force, but there are many whites who are ready to sell whisky to them in time of Indian wars.

The Nez Perces War of 1877, Continued.

(I forgot to mention in a former article that while Joseph and White Bird were considering whether to fight or not, the murderers before mentioned started out and killed settlers right and left. They also murdered some teamsters on or near Salmon river.)

Advancing on Cottonwood.

While the Nez Perces were camped in the pine grove, where the article of last week left them, the chiefs sent two spies toward Cottonwood to see if any soldiers were advancing from that direction. While these spies were concealing themselves on their trip to Cottonwood, they discovered and killed two soldiers. The same day the whole Nez Perces camp mounted, but the camp did not move, except the horsemen who approached Cottonwood. They knew there were soldiers there and they wanted to attack them. Before reaching Cottonwood they ascended a high ridge on the road from Lapwai reservation. Here [t]hey stopped and were looking through their field glasses to see the soldiers at Cottonwood.

Friends and Foes

Suddenly they noticed eleven mounted soldiers at some distance, and in another direction saw some Indians. Joseph immediately dispatched two Indians mounted on their swiftest ponies to ascertain what tribe the Indians belonged to. On reaching them they met Looking Glass and Red Owl, with their little band of men, women and children, nearly all on foot. It will be remembered that Looking Glass drove Joseph and White Bird from his camp and refused to join them in hostilities. After this he had been attacked by the soldiers, his camp destroyed, his stock taken and one woman killed. When the two envoys from the hostiles now reached him he pressed on and reached Joseph and White Bird, who were preparing to charge on the soldiers and citizens at Cottonwood. Looking Glass approached the chief and said:

Looking Glass Joins the Hostiles

"My relations and friends. I had no idea of fighting the white man. My father had traveled many a mile in time of war. My father's warriors fought many battles as allies of the United States soldiers west of the Rocky Mountains. We had friends and relations killed in fighting along with the United States troops. The Indians the troops fought were more our relations than the white man. Why is it that the Nez Perces, having sided with the soldiers in fighting the Cayuses, Yakimas, Umatillas, Spokanes, and others, that to-day I am compelled to raise my hand against the white man? Two days ago my camp was attacked by the soldiers. I tried to surrender in every way I could. My horses, lodges, and everything I had was taken away from me by the soldiers we had done so much for. Now, my people, as long as I live I will never make peace with the treacherous Americans. I did everything I knew to preserve their friendship and be friends with the Americans. What more could I have done? It was because I was too good a friend of theirs that I was attacked. The officer may say it was a mistake. It is a lie. He is a dog, and I have been treated worse than a dog by him. He lies if he says he did not know it was my camp. I am ready for war. Come on and let us attack the soldiers at Cottonwood. Many a man dies for his dear native land, and we might as well die in battle as any other way."

Massacre of a Dispatch Party

During this speech the mounted soldiers who were carrying dispatches were approaching on the Lapwai. Looking Glass after joining the hostiles took command, and an attack was made on the approaching soldiers. The Indians cut them off from Cottonwood, as the soldiers instead of endeavoring to return to that place veered off in another direction, apparently determined to take chances on their horses. Before reaching a high ridge four of the soldiers dismounted and fought bravely. The four who dismounted were all killed by one Indian, a noted warrior named Wat-zam-yas. The other seven were overtaken on the ridge, the principal murderers being in the advance. The soldiers lasted but a few minutes. I did not ascertain how far this was from Cottonwood. In this fight no Indians were killed or wounded. One horse was shot under Wallitze, the warrior who fired the first shot in the war. Another horse was shot under Smoker. White Bird says the soldiers at Cottonwood could have saved this party if they had been brave enough, but they did not even start out from their camp.

The Battles Around Cottonwood

That evening the warriors all returned to their camp. The next day Looking Glass ordered camp to move and be made again in a ravine three or four miles distant from Cottonwood, where there are a few pine trees. As soon as camp was pitched Looking Glass gave orders to the warriors to catch their horses and they would attack the soldiers. Joseph took his Indians and attacked the soldiers, while the rest of the Indians charged on the corrall [sic] and endeavored to capture the horses. But the corrall [sic] was well guarded and defended and they only got twenty-four horses. The soldiers held their position. No Indian was killed in this fight, only one horse being shot under Way-uch-ti-mamy. On the third day the Indians raised camp. While packing up Joseph said to the other chiefs it would be a good plan to pass with their whole camp near Cottonwood, but not to attack the soldiers, and thus entice them out of their breastworks and get them to attack the Indians when they could easily whip them. But unfortunately for the success of this plan some young warriors, without informing the chiefs, had concealed themselves near Cottonwood to attack it.

All this time the Nez Perces believed there was a strong force of soldiers at Cottonwood, and besides, they believed Howard was there. They would rather have him than a hundred soldiers. They wanted Howard badly. The three murderers well knew that whenever the Nez Perces surrendered to Howard they would be the first Indians hung, and what they wanted was to see "the Indian Herder," as they called Howard, and kill him. In fact the great cry in the Nez Perces camp was to kill Howard at first sight. He was the one who got the Indians dissatisfied.

The camp moved as suggested by Joseph but while traveling along and expecting momentarily the Cottonwood garrison to come out and attack them, word was brought that the young warriors who had concealed themselves were already fighting the soldiers. This vexed the chiefs very much and they did not go in that fight. One Indian was killed and two wounded.

The same evening a noted warrior, the same one who killed the four soldiers, took thirty picked warriors, attacked the soldiers in the night and captured 45 head of horses from them, without the loss of a man. Thus ended the Cottonwood battles, only one Indian having been killed and two wounded.

It is a well known fact that when Joseph, White Bird and Looking Glass joined forces they had, all told, just 220 warriors, 25 per cent of whom were armed with only bows and arrows, which are poor weapons against needle guns except in close quarters.

The Nez Perces started from Idaho with 77 lodges. They got 12 more lodges in Bitter Root valley, taking them by force, making 89 lodges in all.

The Nez Perces War of 1877, Continued.

After the fighting in the vicinity of Cottonwood the Nez Perces moved and made camp near Red Owl's farm. Early in the morning the chiefs were told by one of the peaceable Indians that Howard was approaching them with a strong force of soldiers. But they were prepared all this time for Howard's "traps." The camp was in a little ravine. They put up some breastworks on a ridge between their camp and the approaching soldiers. Howard did the same thing. His breastworks were also on a ridge and there was a ravine between the two bodies of fighting men. Howard, with all his military ability, did nothing better than to fire across the ravine to where the Indians were lying behind their defenses. He could have taken the whole camp by storm. The Indians think he well knew it was their determination to have his life, even if they had to charge into the midst of his troops and sacrifice themselves to accomplish their purpose. He knew what would be the result if he exposed himself. I have no wish to say offensive things of Gen'l Howard, but these are the words White Bird said to me sitting by our camp fires in the Sioux camp last summer: "If Howard had been as bold as General Gibbon, we might have been all taken, although we intended to fight to the last."

The Clearwater Battles

During the first day's fighting, there were four Indians killed and four wounded. They fought through the night until daybreak. No Indians were killed in the night fighting. The second day the battle continued the same as the first, but no Indians were killed or wounded. The firing was all at long range. I do not know how many men Howard had in these great battles, but as near as I can ascertain he must have had two or three men to each Indian.

About the middle of the afternoon of the second day's fighting General Looking Glass ordered camp to be moved, and the entire camp was accordingly moved before Howard's eyes. It seems, therefore, that Looking Glass was a better General than Howard, as he withdrew his camp from the front of the enemy and moved away without the loss of either women, children, horses or lodges.

At this time Looking Glass had sole control of the camp, although Joseph ranked as high, or perhaps higher, as chief. Joseph's reason for not leading the camp was that there was more or less discontent and growling among the warriors and Joseph thought he had best have nothing to do with the camp except to follow the movements ordered by Looking Glass. White Bird assisted Looking Glass.

After moving camp they reached a creek near Kamiah where they passed another night, expecting to be attacked by Howard at any moment. But no soldiers appeared. The third day they crossed Clearwater. The river was high. Only about half the camp was across the river when they saw Howard's troops approaching. There was quick work done then. It only took a few minutes to cross the balance of the camp. Shortly after they got across the troops reached the river and tried to cross. But Looking Glass was on the alert, and rallying his warriors opened fire on the soldiers and compelled them to fall back. This ended the great battles of Idaho. Howard could not cross the Clearwater and Looking Glass left the field. It is a well established fact among the Nez Perces that Howard only killed four Nez Perces Indians during his operations in Idaho, and one other killed at Cottonwood foots up the grand total of men killed at five.

The Nez Perces War of 1877, Continued.
On the Trail

After the Idaho battles had ended the Nez Perces camp moved from near Clearwater to a place called Wyap-p. The second day they made camp at a place called Sah-wis-nin-mah. The next day Looking Glass took a portion of the warriors back to harass Howard, and the camp moved but a few miles. Looking Glass did not, however, attack or discover himself to Howard, but made a night raid to capture the horses of the "friendly" Indians who were in Howard's service. They captured and drove away sixty-five head. After reaching camp with them a number of Nez Perces scouts were sent back to look for Howard. They had a very good plan laid to destroy Howard's command, but he did not have nerve to push the Indians. Although they did everything they could to entice him, he was rather shy, and took good care not to follow too closely on the Nez Perces after they got on the Lo Lo trail, always sending his Nez Perces scouts a few days' march ahead of his command.

Capturing and Paroling Prisoners

While Looking Glass' rear guard scouts were watching the trail one day they discovered three Indians following it. These three Indians were scouts for Howard. Unfortunately for them they were surrounded before they knew what to do. Looking Glass' scouts were under command of Watz-am-yas, a brave warrior whom I have before mentioned, an honest, good man as ever lived, and who, like Looking Glass, had used every endeavor to preserve peace. When Howard's scouts were captured, Watz-am-yas addressed the prisoners as follows:

"We are your relations. Your skins, your hair, your bodies, everything you are or have about you are the same as ours. Your supposed friends, that is, the Americans, have marked our native country with the blood of your relations. The white man has been drawing Nez Perces blood for many years. Our chiefs have put all their nerves between their teeth to keep peace with the white man. And yet you are not satisfied with the way in which we have been treated, but are assisting in working against us. We have captured you before and let you go. We knew you had taken up arms against us, but for relations sake we let you go. You promised us before that you would remain at your homes and not help Howard destroy us. Every word you promised us has proved a lie, but we have kept our promises to you, while your promises have been lies. We have spared your lives many times. We will do so again if you promise me one thing, that when we let you go you will return to your homes and never make another move or step to fight your relations now under Looking Glass."

The prisoners replied: "Yes. We are so glad to be allowed to go unharmed we will never make another attempt to pursue you.

You have spared our lives during the battles in our own country and have acted manly with us."

Watz-am-yas said again: "I want you to understand that the next Nez Perces scouts we capture acting under Howard we will kill at once."

Watz-am-yas then took all the cartridges they had and two horses, and told them to go home and never make their appearance again during the war.

An Ambush

After the prisoners had been set at liberty Watz-am-yas moved his band a short distance and concealed themselves to await the approach of the soldiers. Suddenly they discovered some more Indians moving on their trail. These were more of Howard's scouts. Watz-am-yas quickly formed his men in a horse shoe shaped line in the brush and encompassing the trail. When Howard's scouts had fairly entered the ambush, Capt. John, the well-known scout of the General's, exclaimed: "Here are some fresh tracks. Let us go back. There is danger around here."

They turned to retreat, but just as they did so Watz-am-yas opened fire. The brush was, however, so dense that all the army scouts, except one that was dangerously wounded, got away. When Watz-am-yas reached the wounded man the latter said: "Spare my life; I am badly wounded and have news to tell you."

"Yes," replied Watz-am-yas, "we have spared your lives too often. You can tell your news after you get to the happy hunting grounds." With that he put a bullet through the scout's head.

The Nez Perces were nine days in coming from Clearwater to Lo Lo.

The Nez Perces War of 1877, Continued.
The Passage of the Lo Lo Barricades —
Why the Nez Perces Moved "Peaceably if They Might, Forcibly If They Must."

When the Nez Perces camp reached the Hot Springs on the Lo Lo trail, not far from Bitter Root valley, three Indians met them in their camp. One of these Indians was a Nez Perces,

but his home was in the Bitter Root valley. He told Looking
Glass there were some soldiers on the trail watching for them to
come.

The Indian Idea.

Looking Glass said he did not want any troubles on this
side of the Lo Lo range; that he did not want to fight either soldiers or citizens east of the Lo Lo, because they were not the ones
who had fought them in Idaho. The idea among the Indians,
uneducated as they were, was that the people of Montana had
no identity with the people of Idaho, and that they were entirely
separate and distinct, having nothing to do with each other. If
they had to fight they believed it was Idaho people they should
fight, and not Montanians. Looking Glass therefore gave orders
to his warriors that in case they should see any white men, either
citizens or soldiers, on the Lo Lo, not to molest them unless,
as they had compelled him in Idaho, these citizens or soldiers
should compel them to fight in self defense. He said: "We are
going to buffalo country. We want to go through the settlements
quietly. We do not wish to harm any one if we can help it."

The Council With Captain [E. A.] Kinney.

The chief then sent an Indian called John Hill and two others in advance of his camp while coming down the Lo Lo. These
three came to a post of four or five white men. This was Captain
Kinney's camp and this was the night John Hill was arrested and
taken to camp. Hill told Kinney the chiefs had sent him ahead
to ascertain if the Nez Perce camp could pass through peaceably.
Hill was sent back to invite the chiefs to come to the white man's
camp, saying that these white men wished to see the chiefs. This
was on Wednesday. Looking Glass immediately started down
with a band of warriors to meet Capt. Kinney of the volunteers.
When Looking Glass reached Kinney's camp, the chief reiter-
ated to him that he did not wish to harm the whites east of the
Lo Lo mountains; that it was true he had fought the soldiers in
Idaho when he was compelled to; that he did not want to fight
any more, and that he only wanted permission to go through to
buffalo country. At this time the Nez Perces believed that Sitting

Bull still retained possession of the Yellowstone country and that if the soldiers still pursued them they could join Sitting Bull. Kinney replied that he had no authority to treat with them but appointed a council for the next day in the afternoon.

A Tribute to Looking Glass.

By this time Captain [Charles C.] Rawn was preparing in the Lo Lo a splendid trap for Looking Glass and his band. Looking Glass knew nothing about this trap. He only thought the soldiers were camped in the customary manner, and had no idea of entrenchments being prepared to obstruct the passage of himself and warriors. Readers, I do not wish my motives mis-construed in giving Looking Glass the leading position in these movements and councils. I am not censuring Joseph when I do not give him preference, nor am I influenced by kinship with Looking Glass. My statements are simply the truth of history. I know it was understood, and probably is yet, by nearly all that Joseph was the commanding chief of the Nez Perces forces dur-ing the war and that he really is the man who should have credit for the good work in restraining his warriors from excesses in their passage into and through Bitter Root. It is an error. Joseph was a good man but he had nothing to do with the camp, after Looking Glass joined it near Cottonwood, only by following it to shelter himself from the retributive hands of the white man. It was Looking Glass who saved many a white man's life during the campaign; he was commander; as he ordered, camp was moved or remained stationary and what military credit is due for the conduct of that campaign is due to him. Knowing Looking Glass to be well known to many whites, and that he was entitled to his reputation as a really good, kind-hearted Red Man, I submit these facts, incidentally, to correct a popular error. White Bird was a fighting cock, but, with the exception of an instance on Salmon River, he awaited orders from his superior chiefs.

The Councils With Capt. Rawn.

Capt. Rawn's camp, where he had erected rifle pits in the cañon, was about sixteen miles from Missoula and about four miles above the mouth of Lo Lo. The mountains on the south side of Lo Lo are precipitous and densely covered with standing timber, so that escape on that side was impossible. On the north side grassy ridges stretched away from the stream, allowing a passage in almost any direction.

On Thursday Looking Glass and White Bird met Captain Rawn and a few armed men and shook hands with Rawn. Of course the latter wanted the feather in his hat and told Looking Glass he must give up his arms. Captain Rawn and Looking Glass then appointed another day to have a talk.

The Indian Council.

Looking Glass returned to his camp and told his warriors the conditions demanded for them to treat upon. By this time they well knew about "The Corral," as Looking Glass termed Rawn's fortifications. The Indians thought it was ridiculous to give up their arms to their foes. White Bird made a speech and said:

"We remember a big war that took place once on the Columbia river. The United States troops fought against the Yakimas, Kayuses, Umatillas, Spokanes and Coeur d'Alenes. Colonel [George] Wright was the big chief of the soldiers. After many battles the Indians were defeated. Colonel Wright told the Indians that if they would surrender he would treat them well and hurt no one but the murderers. On these conditions the Indians surrendered. Then Col. Wright hung many innocent Indians. Some of them deserved hanging, but many others hands were clear of white men's blood. These soldiers camped below us are of the same kind. How do we know but that Joseph, Looking Glass and others will be hung immediately after we surrender? The officer tells us he does not know who will be hung; that the government has to decide on that question." There were manifestations of approval when White Bird had spoken.

Looking Glass said, "Yes. We do not want to fight. I tried to surrender in Idaho but my offer was rejected. The soldiers came upon my camp and the first thing I knew the bullets were flying around my head. The soldiers lie so that I have no more confidence in them. They have had their way for a long time;

now we must have ours. We must go to buffalo country. If we are not allowed to go peaceably we shall do the best we can. If the officer wishes to build corrals for the Nez Perces he may, but they will not hold us back. We are not horses. The country is large. I think we are as smart as he is and know the roads and mountains as well."

The Last Talk.

The Nez Perces, however, concluded to have another council and try to make peace without giving up their arms — the Indian way of making treaties. On Friday Capt. Rawn made his appearance about a half mile below the Indian village with about 100 men and halted. An Indian by the name of Pierre, a Flathead was sent forward by the officer. When Looking Glass saw so many men near his camp he thought they had certainly come to fight. Looking Glass returned word by Pierre that he would meet Captain Rawn, unarmed, halfway between the forces. The council was held and Looking Glass proposed to surrender all the ammunition of the camp as a guarantee that the Indians intended to go through the country peaceably. When told that nothing but an unconditional surrender would be accepted, he asked for another meeting next day to give him time to consult with the other chiefs. Captain Rawn told him that any further communication he had to make must be made under a flag of truce at the fortified camp.

On considering the matter further the Indians determined not to trust themselves under the condition demanded. They thought perhaps the white man was anxious to make peace, but still they feared treachery. I remember hearing Delaware Jim, the acting interpreter, relate that when Rawn met Looking Glass and demanded the surrender of the Indian guns, Looking Glass replied through the interpreter, "If you want my arms so bad you can start in taking them. I made up my mind before leaving Idaho that we would talk with the white man only through our guns. When I promise I fulfill and do not lie as the white man does. When a Chinaman travels he carries no arms. Do you think

I am a Chinaman? It is foolish to think of a whole camp going to the buffalo country and not carrying a single gun."

Passing the Fort.

On Saturday Looking Glass ordered camp to be raised and directed the women to travel on the north side of Lo Lo until they passed the "Nez Perces Corral," then cross the Lo Lo and turn in a southerly direction up Bitter Root Valley. The warriors were to cover the movement. The camp moved. The soldiers and volunteers got into position in the earthworks and while they were uselessly standing to arms the Indians passed deliberately by without any fight whatever.

While the camp was moving in this manner the Indians captured Henry McFarland, Jack Walsh and another man. These men were volunteers. Looking Glass told them they could go home and attend to their own business. During the day several white men fell into the hands of the Nez Perces, and to all of them Looking Glass repeated the remark, "Go home and mind your own business; we will harm no man."

That evening the Nez Perces made camp on [J. P.] McLain's place, about eight miles above the mouth of Lo Lo, in Bitter Root Valley.

The Nez Perces War of 1877, Continued.

In my last paper, the Nez Perces were left in camp, on the evening of the passage of Lo Lo, about a mile above McLain's ranche, in Bitter Root valley. The same evening W. J. Stephens and about 50 or 60 volunteers reached the camp of Looking Glass. The old chief himself was the first one to meet and speak to them. Some of these volunteers were on their way back to their homes in the Bitter Root valley, and had run into the Nez Perces camp unintentionally. Doubtless some of them thought their lives not very valuable when they found themselves encompassed by the Nez Perces. Looking Glass well knew the facts. He said to them, "You are volunteers; you come over to fight us. I could kill you if I wanted to, but I do not. We have many women and children. I do not care for my own life, but I have pity on them. You can go to your homes. I give you my word of honor that I will harm nobody." After this talk the volunteers dispersed in all directions for their homes.

The Question of Leadership.

I forgot to mention in the preceeding paper that while the Nez Perces were camped on the Lo Lo, above the fortifications, and it was supposed they could not get past "the corral" without surrendering, Joseph said to Looking Glass, "Let us go on. If not allowed to pass, we will fight our way through Lo Lo and next fight our way through Montana. We want peace, but the whites want us to be kept in the Lo Lo cañon. Let us go through the best way we can, whether it is by peace or war."

Looking Glass answered: "Did you, or did you not, with other chiefs, elect me for leader through this country, because I knew it and the people, and did you not promise that I should have the whole command and do as I please? You and the other chiefs told me these words. Now, Joseph, I wish to know if you are going to break your promise. If you are anxious to fight I will withdraw my people and you can fight as pleases you. I fight when I cannot avoid it, but not otherwise. Still I can fight my battles as well as anybody. At the fortifications in our way there are some Flatheads aiding the whites. If we fight the whites we must fight the Flatheads. Some of them are our relations. Now you can make your choice."

Joseph replied: "You are right, Looking Glass. We did elect you head man of the camp. Go ahead and do the best." So Looking Glass remains in supreme command.

The Mysterious "Three Indians."

About this same time three Nez Perces arrived at the Flathead agency. They came direct from the Yellowstone country *via* Missoula. Eagle-of-the-Light was at that time camped at Flathead agency, and they came here to see him and exchange news. These three Indians had been acting as scouts for General [Nelson A.] Miles, looking after Sitting Bull Sioux on the

Yellowstone, but while on a scout in that valley they were told by some white men that the Nez Perces had broken out in Idaho, and they deserted Miles to go to their homes in Idaho. The name of the head man of these three was Grizzly Bear Youth. He acted like a grizzly bear in the Big Hole Battle. This man had many engagements with the Sioux and always got away with the white feather. When he learned the hostile Nez Perces were on the Lo Lo trail he remained at the agency waiting for them to pass Missoula county. He was at the agency about one week. The news reached Missoula that these three Indians were at the agency obtaining cartridges from the trader, Duncan McDonald, and it caused quite a disturbance of public feeling. But it was an error. These three men had a pack mule, but it was for their blankets and cooking utensils and not to pack cartridges. Duncan McDonald knows better than to let hostile Indians have cartridges. During the stay here of Grizzly Bear Youth he found how near this point is to the National Boundary line, and he thought he would go over to Lo Lo and see Looking Glass and tell him. Grizzly Bear Youth was, however, one of Lawyer's Nez Perces, was rich in horses, and desired himself to get back to the reserve in Idaho, for even before this he tried to go through by the other route, but after reaching Horse Plains, 45 miles from the agency, he turned back, thinking it was not safe to attempt to get through that way. Duncan McDonald told him he had better go by Lo Lo trail and surrender to Howard.

Accordingly, the three Nez Perces started from the agency, on Sunday afternoon, for the Lo Lo trail. Before leaving, Grizzly Bear Youth said here that if he should see Looking Glass he would try to influence the Nez Perces to go through the Flathead reservation to Tobacco Plains and not through the settlements of the Territory. When he reached Lo Lo, he found that the Nez Perces camp was only a few miles above, and he concluded he might go over and see his relations, although he did not purpose [propose] to join the camp. Before dismounting from his horse he told the chiefs they were a band of fools; that it was folly for a handfull [sic] of Indians to think of fighting the United States government. After dismounting he went to Looking Glass and White Bird and told them what he thought it best for them to do, — that was to turn back and go by the Flathead reservation and Flathead Lake to the British possessions.

The Route Determined Upon.

Looking Glass then called a council and told Joseph and the others what Grizzly Bear Youth had said. White Bird and Red Owl agreed; they wanted to go by the reserve. Joseph did not say a word. Looking Glass wanted to go by Big Hole and down the Yellowstone and join the Crows, according to agreement, became the Crows had promised them that whenever the Nez Perces fought the whites they would join them. There was a disagreement, but after quarrelling [sic] among themselves they concluded it was best to let Looking Glass have his way. This council was held about a mile or a mile and a half above McLain's ranch, on the Bitter Root.

The Nez Perces War of 1877, Continued.

Before continuing this narrative I desire to mention Captain Rawn's connection with the passage of the Lo Lo fortifications. It has been discussed whether he acted cowardly or not in permitting the Nez Perces to pass. The Nez Perces gave him credit for wisdom in not opening fire on them. The bravest of their warriors would have done the same. Had he attacked them he would have been severely whipped. It is a well known fact that the biggest "Indian eaters" at Lo Lo were less courageous than those who professed less.

Nearly a Fight.

When the Indians were marching past the fortifications and down Lo Lo, the voice of Looking Glass could be distinctly heard addressing his warriors: "Don't shoot, don't shoot. Let the white men shoot first." This he repeated over and over. All this time the soldiers and volunteers kept their positions in the breastworks. When the volunteers saw that Captain Rawn would not fire on the Indians, some of them started down the stream to head them off. Looking Glass was on the alert for a movement of this

kind, and placed his best warriors between the volunteers and his
women, children and pack-horses — in fact, as they passed down
the women and children were advanced ahead and the warriors
held back to act as a rear guard. As they were moving down Lo Lo
they saw these volunteers dashing down Lo Lo with the evident
purpose of cutting off the women and children. At the sight of
this the warriors believed certainly that they were going to have
a fight, and started with a yell in the direction of the volunteers.
Capt. Rawn, seeing the demonstrations of the volunteers, and
believing a collision was likely to occur between them and the
Nez Perces, dispatched a half-breed named A[lexander] Matte
and a few Flatheads to ascertain whether a fight occurred and to
report to him immediately. While Matte and his Flatheads were
proceeding down Lo Lo they met John Scott riding rapidly back
toward Rawn's camp. He had his hat in his hand using it as a whip
and his war horse was putting in his best licks. On meeting Matte
he told him an engagement was going on — that the volunteers
were fighting. He wanted Matte to turn back lest he should be
killed. But Matte kept on as he was ordered by Rawn, who desired
to reinforce the volunteers if they engaged the Nez Perces. Matte
came in sight of the volunteers just as the Nez Perces warriors
started for them. The Indian eaters thought sure they had seen
their last day, and stampeded up Lo Lo toward Rawn's camp. A
few halted when they had gone a little distance or when they had
reached Matte and the Flatheads. Looking Glass and his warriors
had swift horses and could have intercepted them in their line of
retreat and in case of a fight would have cut them off from Rawn,
and had the two parties at their mercy. The builders of the Lo Lo
fortifications may have thought they were a shelter; but they were
mistaken. The rifle pits were exposed on one side, and on that
side there was a steep mountain, covered with trees, fallen timber
and rocks, affording excellent cover for the Indian sharpshooters,
from which they could have picked off those in the rifle pits at
their leisure. It is true that there were a few splendid shots in the
force, but two-thirds of them were not, and all the Indians were
hunters, experienced fighters and good marksmen.

What Might Have Been.

I remember White Bird said that if war had opened on Lo Lo the whole country would have been fired, and many a farmer would have lost his crops and home and perhaps his scalp. It is probable that they would then have moved north through the Flathead reservation. Whatever the chiefs of the Reserve and Bitter Root valley may have said about the peaceable disposition of their Indians, and that there was no danger of their joining the Nez Perces was a mistake. There were Indians on the Bitter Root and Flathead reserve who had their guns ready for use if a battle occurred at Lo Lo. Indians had been whispering at these places long before the hostiles reached Lo Lo. The writer of these papers stated in Missoula before ever Walatze, Tap-sis-il-pilp and Um-till-lip-cown raised their hands in Idaho that a Nez Perces war would soon break out in that Territory. His prediction was laughed at. Who would believe that the Nez Perces would take to the war-path? The situation was but little less threatening with some of the Flatheads and Pen d'Oreilles in Missoula county.

After raising camp at McLain's there was still some discussion as to the route to be taken — whether to the British Possessions through the Flathead reservation, or to the Yellowstone *via* the Big Hole. If forced to fight they proposed to join the Sioux or Crows in the Yellowstone country; if not, they designed after getting their dried meat to return to Idaho the next Spring. Finally Looking Glass urged that he wanted to go by Big Hole, because he knew the country better, and although this was only a pretext, as they could have found their way just as well northward, his wishes were respected and they started up Bitter Root.

Charlos' Greeting.

On reaching the place of Charlos, the Flathead chief, Looking Glass summoned a number of his warriors to accompany him to visit Charlos and inquire of him where the best place to camp was to find good grass. On approaching Charlos' house Looking Glass thought it would be honorable to extend his hand to Charlos before making his inquiry. But Charlos refused to accept the extended hand, saying, "Why should I shake hands with men whose hands are bloody? My hands are clean of blood." Looking Glass replied: "Your hands are as red with the blood of your enemies as mine are. Why should my hands be clean when I have been forced to fight the white man? Your hands are as bloody as ours. I did not come to talk about blood. I came to ask you the best place to camp." Charlos answered: "Above my house is the best spot to camp," and there they accordingly pitched their tents.

At Stevensville.

Looking Glass kept close watch of his warriors while camped near Stevensville, in which town they did considerable trading. He sent several to camp for being disorderly. It was very fine for the officers sitting in camp and indulging in strong drink to condemn the people of Stevensville for selling these Indians goods and provisions, and allege that they were aiding the Nez Perces to recruit for their march, and that they should be punished therefor. This talk was something like Howard's. Their words have more force than their deeds. These Nez Perces would never stand before a little town like Stevensville and perish of starvation when plenty could be had there. The Nez Perces under Looking Glass offered to buy from them first, but if they had been refused and obliged to resort to that measure they would have plundered. Had as many soldiers as there were men been stationed in Stevensville, and a band of starving Nez Perces like these been refused food, the soldiers with all the laws of the United States on their side would have lasted but a short time. It was fortunate for Stevensville that citizens and not soldiers had possession of it. Under the circumstances the citizens of Stevensville did right.

Ordered Out of Camp.

An incident happened during the time of the encampment near Stevenville that illustrates the indisposition of the Nez Perces to have any conflict with the people of Montana. A citizen wished to visit the Indian camp. He mounted his best riding horse, and,

Chief Charlo

Source: Montana Historical Society Photograph Archives, Helena, Montana,
detail of 954-526, photograph by John K. Hillers, Bureau of American
Ethnology, Washington, D.C., 1884.

accompanied by a half breed who had presented Looking Glass with fifty pounds of flour, rode thereto. It should be remembered that Looking Glass had no lodge nor even cooking utensils. He camped in the open air and received his meals from his warriors. He was so glad to receive as a visitor the half breed who had presented him with the sack of flour, that he invited him to have a smoke. He noticed the actions of the citizen and told him there was a certain portion of the camp which it would be best for him not to visit — that some of their relations had been killed in Idaho, and it was not best for him to go near them. The citizen, however, wanted to trade off his horse for a fortune, and went charging around the camp promiscuously, making his steed prance and caper, and asking the Nez Perces three of their good horses for his one. He had many good offers to trade, but always refused. In any other camp than the Nez Perces he would have been packed off, and that would have been the last of him and his funny horse. In one of his circuits he went to that part of the camp which he had been advised by Looking Glass to avoid. A wounded Nez Perces, some of whose relations had been killed in Idaho, was standing by a log and resting on his gun. On seeing the white man cavorting around in an impudent way, the Indian said in English, "Me give you three horses; my horses very good one." The white man refused. It seemed that he only wanted to put on style. This made the warrior angry and he exclaimed, "You go home, you d—n white man; you ——." It was a wonder he was not killed. But he left hastily, and if that funny horse of his had a 1:40 gait in him, it was brought out as the citizen lit out for Stevensville.

The Lockwood Affair.

Not being acquainted with the country above Stevensville, I am unable to designate the other camping places. An incident, however, occurred near the head of Bitter Root valley, at [Myron M.] Lockwood's ranch, I believe, which I wish to relate. A certain band of the Nez Perces were under command of T-whool-we-tzoot, the same Indian who was made prisoner by Howard in Idaho when he was elected Speaker of the tribe at the council.

This was the worst band in the whole camp, and a very unruly lot. While passing Lockwood's ranch, some of this band went into the cabin and helped themselves to about 200 pounds of flour, 30 or 40 pounds of coffee, one file, two or three shirts, and some other small articles. On reaching camp they went to Looking Glass and told him what they had done. Looking Glass was very angry and told T-whool-we-tzoot that unless they obeyed his orders they should be put out of the camp. He said he would not permit plundering, and demanded seven head of horses from those Indians as payment for the articles they had stolen. The thieves consented to give up seven head of horses and leave them at the ranch, but Looking Glass would not be satisfied until they branded the horses with Lockwood's brand and left them at his ranch. I understand that Lockwood, not satisfied with the seven horses left him, went on the war path, joined [Gen. John] Gibbon's command, got shot at the Big Hole battle and lost his brother at the same place.

The Nez Perces War of 1877, Continued.

While traveling slowly toward Big Hole, dragging their lodge poles, White Bird went to Looking Glass and said:

White Bird Urges Expedition.

"Why do you allow the camp to drag lodge poles? By the way you are acting you seem to anticipate no danger. How do we know but that some of these days or nights we shall be attacked by the whites. We should be prepared for trouble. Let your lodge poles be destroyed and move as rapidly as possible without them to the buffalo plains."

Looking Glass answered: "That is all nonsense and bosh. Who is going to trouble us? What wrong did we do in passing through the Bitter Root settlements? I think that we did very well in going through the country peaceably with a band of hostiles like we have got. We are in no hurry. The little bunch of soldiers from Missoula are not fools enough to attack us. We had best take the world as easily as possible. We are not fighting with the people of this country."

White Bird replied: "Well, it is no harm to be prepared. We know the whites want us to surrender our arms to them. We were told while in the Bitter Root valley there were soldiers and volunteers all over the country, in front and rear, looking for us. If they want us to surrender our arms to them they will have to fight for them."

Looking Glass said, "Oh, there is no danger."

"All right," replied White Bird.

The Medicine Man Speaks.

Another Indian, well known among themselves as a "medicine man," said to the chiefs a day before the battle of Big Hole, "What are we doing here?" After singing his song he continued, "While I slept my medicine told me to move on, that Death is approaching us. Chief, I only tell you this because it may be of some good to this camp. If you take my advice we can avoid death, and that advice is to speed through this country. If not, there will be tears in our eyes in a short time."

Indian Beliefs.

Now, reader, let me explain about Indian "medicine." The Indian's belief may seem ridiculous to civilized people, but the Indians believe in their "medicine" as implicitly as Ignatius Loyola or the Jesuits believed or believe in Christ, or a Chinaman believes in Confucius. The Indian medicine man goes to the mountains and starves himself for several days to obtain his "medicines." So long as his stomach contains any food whatever he can obtain no "medicine." His system must be purified from all edible matter, his body must be made clean by ablutions, and he must have faith that his desires for "medicine" will be granted. These "medicines" are chiefly beasts, fowls, insects and fishes of all kinds, which come to him and tell him what is going to happen. It seems the Spiritualists have somewhat similar beliefs.

I am not speaking of the semi-civilized tribes, but of the native Indians in their wildest state. Their superstition on this point has cost many a life. The writer of these papers has had many difficulties because he does [not] choose to believe in what the medicine men say. It is not strange. A man in the South of

Ireland who abused a priest might be killed by some devout believer. The Indians are as fixed in their belief in the medicine man. I do not ask readers to believe as they do; I am, however, explaining a matter that has a great deal to do with the actions of Indians. [The next week on January 31, 1879, Mills published a correction: "In this his statement was reversed. It should have read, 'The writer of these papers had had many difficulties because he does *not* choose to believe,' etc."]

What They Knew of Pursuit.

When the medicine man had advised the chiefs what to do, Looking Glass, although he protested his inability to see where danger was to come from, ordered camp to be moved forward, and *they camped that night on the Big Hole battle ground.* The Nez Perces say they had seen white men moving down the distant hills. These were some of [Lt. James H.] Bradley's scouts, who have believed they were not discovered by the Indians. They gave the matter little attention. They thought they were merely scouts watching their movements, a surveillance to which they had become accustomed, and they knew that the little band of soldiers that had tried to bar their passage of the Lo Lo was following them. They did not know this little band had been reinforced by Gibbon's command from Fort Shaw. They had no idea they would be attacked by the Lo Lo soldiers.

"There Was a Sound of Revelry," Etc.

On the night they camped at the battle ground the most of the warriors were up until a late hour engaged in their war dance. This caused a deep sleep to fall on them after they went to their lodges. Some of them slept so soundly they never awakened. The camp, not apprehending danger, was sleeping soundly, when suddenly the rifles of the soldiers belched forth their deadly fire, and the camp was awakened to find their enemies plunging through it dealing death and destruction in every direction. General Gibbon had all the advantage of a complete surprise.

The Rout and the Rally.

With the soldiers in the midst of their camp before they were even awakened, those who could fled to the brush along the brook. Here it was that White Bird and Looking Glass displayed the valor of true chieftains, rallied their warriors from a rout, and plucked a victory from the very jaws of defeat. White Bird was the first to rally his warriors to a charge upon the soldiers. "Why are we retreating?" he shouted in Nez Perces. "Since the world was made brave men fight for their women and children. Are we going to run to the mountains and let the whites kill our women and children before our eyes? It is better we should be killed fighting. Now is our time; fight! These soldiers cannot fight harder than the ones we defeated on Salmon river and in White Bird Cañon. Fight! Shoot them down. We can shoot as well as any of these soldiers." At these words the warriors wheeled around and started back to fight the soldiers in their camp.

Looking Glass was at the other end of the camp. His voice was heard calling out, "Wallitze! Tap-sis-ill-pilp! Um-til-lilp-cown! this is a battle! These men are not asleep as were those you murdered in Idaho! These soldiers mean battle. You tried to break my promise at Lo Lo. You wanted to fire at the fortified place. Now is the time to show your courage and fight. You can kill right and left. I would rather see you killed than the rest of the warriors, for you commenced the war. Now, go ahead and fight." The warriors addressed were so angered and aroused they did not care for their lives, and rallied to the charge with those led by White Bird. Some of them said they had heard the white man was a good fighter, but he seemed to fight best when his enemy was asleep.

Death of Two Instigators.

Many women and children were killed before getting out of their beds. In one lodge there were five children. One soldier went into it and killed every one of them. When the warriors rallied and opened fire they poured their shot into the soldiers so rapidly and effectually that they suffered considerable loss and soon retreated to a point of timber near the trail. In the midst of the hottest of the fight Tap-sis-ill-pilp was killed. Wallitze, on being told his companion was dead, ran right into the soldiers and was shot down dead in his tracks. Thus did two of the three

General John Gibbon

Source: Library of Congress, Photograph Division, Washington, D.C.,
DIG-cwpb-04455.

murderers who brought on the war expiate their offense, and it is due to them to say that they died as brave as the bravest.

Death of Captain [William] Logan.

Before these two men were killed an episode of interest occurred at the lodges. In a fight between an officer and a warrior, the warrior was shot down dead. The warrior's sister was standing by him when he fell, and as he lay there his six-shooter lay by his side. The woman seeing her brother dying and the blood running from his mouth, seized the six-shooter, leveled it at the officer, fired, shot him through the head and killed him. From all the information I can obtain, I believe the officer was Captain Logan.

A Personal Encounter.

While the soldiers were retreating across to the timber, Grizzly Bear Youth followed them and was doing rapid work with his Henry rifle. If I remember correctly the description there was a crossing or slough the soldiers had to go over that impeded them. While the soldiers were at this place a volunteer turned around and commenced damning the Indians lustily. He is described as a tall, ugly looking man, and I will describe the incident following as it was related to me by Grizzly Bear Youth last summer at the Sioux camp near Fort Walsh:

"When I was following the soldiers, trying to kill as many of them as possible, a big, ugly volunteer turned around swearing and made for me. I suppose he had no time to load his needle gun, so he swung it over his head by the barrel and rushed at me to strike me over the head with the butt end. I did the same thing. We both struck and each received a blow on the head. The volunteer's gun put a brand on my forehead that will be seen as long as I live. My blow on his head made him fall on his back. I jumped on him and tried to hold him down. The volunteer was a powerful man. He turned me over and got on top. He got his hand on my throat and commenced choking me. I was almost gone and had just strength left to make signs to a warrior, who was coming up, to shoot him. This was Red Owl's son, who ran up, put his needle gun to the volunteer's side and fired. The ball passed through him and killed him. But I had my arm around the waist of the man when the shot was fired, and the ball after going through the volunteer broke my arm."

This was the second scuffle G. B. Y. had in the Big Hole battle. The other man was a soldier, but he did not last long.

The Warfare Condemned.

I dissent from the plea that the women had to be shot because they fought as well as the men. It was shameful the way women and children were shot down in that fight. The five children I mentioned were sleeping when they were killed. It was reported Sergeant [Mildon H.] Wilson killed nine Indians. Yes: nine women and children. I understand he received a medal from the Government for his bravery at Big Hole. Instead of receiving a medal he should have been court-martialed. It is a well-known fact that the command wasted more powder and lead on the women and children than on the warriors. There were seventy-eight Indians, all told, killed in the Big Hole battle. Of these only thirty were warriors. The others were women and children. About forty women and children were piled up in one little ravine where they had run for shelter. Many women, with from one to three children in their arms, were found dead in that ravine. Some of the children had their mother's breasts in their mouths when both were found there dead. What reason could the soldiers have had to kill them? Had the warriors been with them we might have believed the soldiers could not help it. A daughter of Looking Glass, now north of the line, had hundreds of bullets whiz past her while crawling with a child in her arms to find shelter. The gallant Seventh Infantry! It should be called the Cursed Seventh! They were not satisfied in killing Indians whom they found asleep. They must kill women and children, too. Why, if they wanted to kill women, did they not kill the woman who killed Capt. Logan? It is said she was killed on the spot. It is a lie. I do not even blame her. Any woman would have done the same. There was her brother dying at her feet, his loaded revolver lying by his side. What sister would not have seized it and avenged her brother's death?

[In a subsequent issue on January 31, 1879, MacDonald revised this statement: "And here I wish to make a correction. In my article last week I stated that the woman who shot Captain Logan escaped unharmed. In this I was mistaken. She was killed on the spot by a soldier."]

The Dismounted Howitzer.

While the fight was going on in the morning some of the Nez Perces noticed the howitzer approaching the battle ground. They charged upon the squad with it, killing, I believe, the man in command. After capturing the howitzer they damaged it so that, as they believed, it could not be used. A few minutes later an Indian reached the gun and expressed great regrets that it was rendered useless. He said: "It is a great pity. I know how to use this kind of guns. I learned when I was with Col. Wright fighting Cayuses and Yakimas."

News From a Prisoner.

According to White Bird's statement, Gibbon's command retreated to a high point and intrenched itself. It was thereby saved temporarily, but White Bird did not deem the place impregnable. It was another circumstance [that] saved Gibbon — the Indians were informed Howard's command was close up on their trail, and that volunteers were coming from the eastern part of the Territory. They continued to harass Gibbon, and would have stayed with him till they wore him out had they not been apprehensive of his receiving reinforcements. They got their news in this way: About the time the main fight was over and the warriors were examining their dead, they discovered a white man, a citizen, breathing, with his eyes closed and pretending to be dead, although he was not even wounded. When they found he was "playing 'possum" they took hold of his arms and raised him up. Finding the Indians were too smart to let him get away he jumped to his feet. Looking Glass ordered the warriors not to kill him, saying that he was a citizen, and they might obtain information from him concerning Howard, etc. They then questioned him, and in reply he said Howard would be there in a short time, and that plenty of volunteers were coming from Virginia [City] to head them off. While he was telling the news a woman who had lost her brother and some of her children in the fight came up. She was crying at the time, and on seeing the citizen slapped him in the face. On receiving the blow he instantly gave her a vigorous kick with his boot. He had not more than kicked her when some of the warriors killed him. He would not have been killed had he refrained from kicking her. His statement decided them to raise camp and move on to a more secure place.

White Bird says the volunteers fought better than the regular soldiers, but it was a shame for the Bitter Root volunteers, after the Nez Perces had treated them so well, to join Gibbon and fight them. A white man must have no respect for himself. It makes no difference how well he is treated by the Indians, he will take the advantage. The Nez Perces felt that they behaved themselves while passing through the Bitter Root, and now feel sorer toward the people of that valley than they do toward the soldiers.

The officer remembered as having acted most manly in the Big Hole fight is Capt. [George L.] Browning. He stopped his soldiers from killing two women in front of him.

The Nez Perces War of 1877, Continued.

The Nez Perces were crippled more in the Big Hole battle by General Gibbon, than in any battle before or after. It was in this fight they lost their best warriors.

The Birch Creek Massacre.

The particulars of the killing of the murderers of the Hayden party and the ranchmen at Horse Prairie and Birch Creek are not generally known to the Nez Perces. After numerous inquiries, I find there were two men killed at one place. One of them was murdered in his cabin and the other while endeavoring to escape from the cabin. It must be remembered the Nez Perces were actuated at this time to commit murders by a spirit of revenge. They had just met with a considerable loss in the battle of the

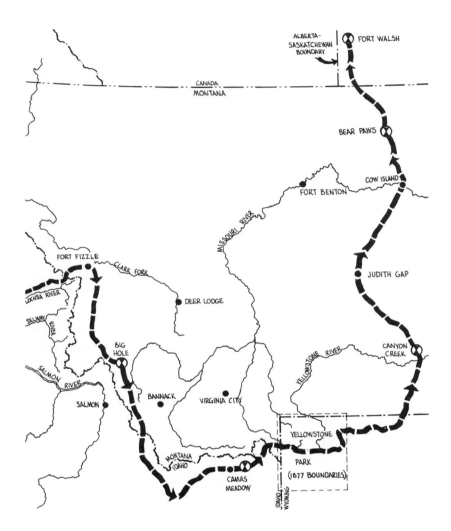

Route of the Nez Perce

Source: John D. McDermott, *Forlorn Hope: The Battle of White Bird Canyon
and the Beginning of the Nez Perce War* (Boise: Idaho State Historical Society,
1978), p. 130

Big Hole, and felt that every white man in their path was their enemy, and by taking his life they could thereby avenge the death of their comrades. After the battle with Gibbon's command the march was resumed. The Indians first came in contact with a party in which there were several white men and two China-men. The exact number of whites is not known, but it is thought the number did not exceed six. The party had wagons and a lot of mules, and the Indians came upon them while they were in camp; the Indian camp was made near the train. The whites had in their possession some whisky which they proposed trading to the Indians for articles of which they stood in need. While the trade was in progress, it began to grow dark. This suited the young and reckless Indians and, as soon as it was dark they pro-ceeded to help themselves. Under the influence, and stimulated by copious draughts of the intoxicant, their hatred to the white race was intensified and they fired their guns into the train. As soon as the firing was begun the whites and Chinamen beat a retreat. I say they "beat a retreat." The Indians did not make an examination to find whether or not they had killed any of the party, but after the volley they approached and rifled the train, taking all the articles in the wagons and camp. They also took the animals. This ended the fight at this place. The place at which this occurred is not known to either the Indians or the writer. As has been stated, the route was new and unknown to the Indians. (In a note to this article Mr. McDonald says: Following is the language of my informant: "We did not ask the whites under whose command they were. The fact they they were under com-mand of Hayden was of no interest to us. All we wanted was the whisky in their possession. Once that was obtained, the appro-priation of the rest of the possessions was merely a question of time. An Indian under the influence of whisky has no more sense than a white man when drunk, and is not any more responsible for his actions. When an Indian is drunk he will commit crimes he would not think of when sober. As an evidence of the truth of this statement, I have only to say that while under the influence of the whisky captured from the train one of the bravest and best warriors in the Nez Perces band was killed and another narrowly escaped death at the hands of their comrades.")

More Medicine.

While the Nez Perces camp was moving beyond Camas Meadow, two days ahead of Howard's command, Grizzly Bear Youth lay in his tent, suffering from the wounds received in the Big Hole fight. Here a great bird, that never alights on the earth or trees, but rests only in the clouds, appeared to the sufferer in his lodge. In regard to this bird it is claimed by the Nez Perces to live in their country; that it is never seen except by those wishing it for their "Medicine." They also say it is much larger and far superior to the game eagle, and will pick up game of any kind and fly with it. This bird was the "Medicine" of Grizzly Bear Youth, who was awakened from a troubled sleep into which he had fallen by the voice of the bird, which said: "I see you have tears in your eyes, caused by grieving over the loss of your relatives, your country and your arm. Why do you cry? Look behind about two days' travel and you will see two creeks. These creeks are at Camas Meadow. The big chief of the Idaho soldiers, "Cut Arm," and his force are camped there. It is rather a strong force, but fear them not. The Nez Perces will kill some of his men and get possession of his animals. There are two kinds of animals in the camp. I can tell you the name of only one kind. This kind is horses. The others differ from the horse in many ways. Now I must leave you. You may rely on what I have told you. Good luck to you." The bird then disappeared.

Imparting the Knowledge.

It is customary for Indians, when they have received news from their "Medicine," to summon all their brethren and inform them of what they have been told. Grizzly Bear Youth sent for the warriors, who came to his lodge. After singing his medicine song, he told the Indians of the news he had received from his "Medicine," the Air Bird. He told them that next night Cut Arm's (Cut Arm is Howard) animals would be in their possession. One-half of the animals were horses; the other half he could not describe.

He further said, "I want all the warriors to go back to Camas Meadow to-morrow evening."

An Attack Agreed Upon.

When the talk at Grizzly Bear Youth's lodge was over the warriors retired and the camp was soon quiet. While they slept two scouts, who had been sent to look for Howard's command, returned to the camp. They immediately went to Looking Glass and told him that Howard would camp next day at Camas Meadow, and that he had with him a large pack-train. Looking Glass at once summoned the Nez Perces and told them that he wanted the warriors, with the exception of twenty-five, who were to remain under charge of White Bird to guard the camp, to get ready to go and attack Howard. Accordingly, about two hundred and twenty-five warriors, under command of Looking Glass and Joseph, left the camp next morning. They sent scouts all over the country, and traveling slow, reached Howard's camp about midnight. The Indians were told not to approach the camp until so ordered by Looking Glass, who first sent spies to examine the location, etc. The report made to the camp showed that there were two creeks, about three hundred yards apart. Howard's command crossed both creeks and went into camp. The Virginia [City] volunteers made their camp before crossing the second creek. The night was so dark the spies had not discovered the volunteer camp, and they were under the impression that their enemies were all with Howard. It was very lucky indeed for the volunteers that their presence was not known.

Getting Ready.

Looking Glass on learning the situation thought it best to have no fight. He told the warriors he only wanted to capture the stock and that they were to make no move until so ordered by him. A short time before daybreak he gave the order to approach the camp. In obeying a death-like stillness was observed. The Indians made their way on their hands and knees. Howard's pickets could be heard conversing in a low tone of voice. The Indians afterward said they could have captured all the cavalry horses if they had only known where they were, but the night was so dark

that they feared the reports of the spies might be incorrect, and
they were consequently in doubt as to the real position of the soldiers. After getting close to the camp, Looking Glass ordered his
men to prepare for a charge; told them if they could capture the
animals without fighting it would be the better way, as he only
wanted the animals. He also said: "We know American horses are
afraid of Indians; make all the noise you possibly can, as by so
doing we may be able to stampede the whole herd at once."

The Charge.

The order to charge was given, and the work of stampeding
the stock commenced. Ever and anon the voice of Looking Glass
could be heard, calling on the Indians to pay no heed to the soldiers, but secure the horses. His men obeyed his commands and
rent the air with the most hideous yells. They succeeded in capturing over two hundred head of animals — one-half of which were
mules. (These latter were the ones which the "Medicine" Bird
could not describe). While driving the herd a short distance from
the scene of attack, some soldiers were discovered in pursuit. The
first thought was that Howard's command was after them, but
it subsequently proved to be only a small body of cavalry. These
were the troops which were subject to the "whitewashing" process
in the newspapers — Captain [Randolph] Norwood's command,
I believe. Looking Glass ordered the stolen animals to be left in
charge of three warriors, and the rest of his force to conceal themselves. He said, "Let the fool in command of the soldiers come
up to us. Does he think he can take these animals from us with
the force he has? Make haste and hide yourselves." The Indian
force was divided and two lines formed, the warriors concealing
themselves behind trees, rocks, etc. Looking Glass wanted Norwood to advance between the lines formed, but the officer was
too wary to be drawn into the trap. He stationed his men some
distance away and commenced firing. Looking Glass ordered his
men not to fire; that he thought the soldiers had not yet seen
them and were only firing by guess-work. The troops failing to
advance, orders were given to the Indians to fire, and the fight
commenced. The Indians endeavored to get the soldiers between

the lines formed, and had they succeeded, there would have been a massacre similar to that when Custer's command were killed by Sitting Bull and his warriors. The Indians finally made a charge and the troops retreated to a point of timber. While here the Nez Perces became uneasy lest Howard's command should have heard the firing and reinforce the troops under Norwood. Joseph and Looking Glass held a consultation, and as they had suffered no loss whatever, they started back to their camp.

This ended the great battle of Camas Meadow. About noon the Indians halted and Looking Glass divided the stolen animals among his warriors.

The Nez Perces War of 1877, Continued.
Capture of [John] Shively.

In traveling through the country after the capture of Howard's animals at Camas Meadow, the Nez Perces captured a white man in the Lower Geyser Basin. He was engaged in eating his meal when the Indians discovered him. Four of them went up to the man, the rest remaining some distance away. The white man was so astonished at the appearance of the Indians he apparently did not know what to do. He asked the Indians to what tribe they belonged. They answered that they were Sioux, just for the purpose of seeing what the man would say. They then held a council and determined to take the man to their camp and ask for information as to the road to the plains. On reaching camp the prisoner was asked his business in that part of the country, etc. On being told that he was on his way to the settlements in Montana, and that he was familiar with the different routes, they determined to keep him for a guide until they would be in a portion of country known to them. It was also determined that he should be well paid for his services, and that he should not be harmed. Had the prisoner claimed that he did not know the country, he would undoubtedly have been permitted to depart unmolested. But the route they were on was not known by an Indian in the camp, and it was determined to keep the prisoner for a guide. After going into camp for the night, Looking Glass sent for Poker Joe, to whom he said: "You let the white man remain with you and treat him well. You understand how to speak English, and you and the guide can get along well together." It was Poker Joe who first proposed that the prisoner should be kept and made to act as guide. His proposition was made to Looking Glass, White Bird and Joseph, and they concluded to accept Poker Joe's advice. When the camp moved the next day the prisoner was ordered to ride behind an Indian. His property was appropriated by the others, who intended returning it when his services were no longer required. The Indians all speak highly of the prisoner, as he was always willing to do whatever he was asked. Poker Joe told the man he must not attempt to escape, and that he would be his friend. At the time of his escape the Indians intended keeping him but one day longer. They then proposed returning the property taken from him and paying him for his trouble. It may be thought by some that this would not have been done, but White Bird told the writer that they intended to do right by the prisoner and pay him liberally for his services. We believe the prisoner's name was Shively.

Capture of the Radersburg Party.

Early next morning after the capture of Shively some of the young warriors captured a party of eight persons — six men and two women. The party were in their tents asleep when the Indians came up, except two men who were building a fire. The ladies were both young. The party had a wagon and a buggy. The appearance of the Indians aroused the rest of the party, and they at once made preparations to leave without getting their breakfast. Seeing this, they were told by an Indian that they need not fear, that they were friends of the whites, and that he himself would escort them safely through the Indian camp, and they could then return to their homes unmolested. The preparations to start were soon made, but they had proceeded but a short distance when they were surrounded by a large party of warriors, who told them it was not safe for them to travel on that road, as there were bad Indians behind who would kill them. The Indians then had a talk, and it was concluded to take the captured

party to the chiefs in order to see whether or not they be permitted to return, and the party was ordered to march toward the
camp. After traveling some distance up the east bank of Fire Hole
River the wagon and carriage had to be abandoned on account
of the fallen timber. The horses were unhitched and saddles put
on them for the women. While the horses were being unsaddled,
one of the white men (Frank Carpenter) requested permission
to go to Looking Glass and see if he would not permit them to
go home. Permission being granted, he hired an Indian for six
needle-gun cartridges to conduct him to the chief, who was in
camp at the foot of a steep mountain, just west of Mary's Lake.
Carpenter shook hands with Looking Glass, and while talking
with him Poker Joe accompanied by Shively came up. Joe invited
Carpenter to accompany him to his lodge, and on reaching there
plied him [with] questions as to who were members of his party,
where they were from, etc. He answered all the questions, and
then asked if they could not go home. Poker Joe replied: "Yes, no
kill citizens; kill Lewiston soldiers all the time."

In the meantime the other captives were hurried forward
until they came to the Nez Perces camp. They were then told by
Poker Joe that they could return, but they must leave their horses, arms and ammunition; that he would give them other horses
to ride home, and also give them other guns and three cartridges
each. This he did according to his word. At this juncture Looking Glass ordered camp to be raised and the march resumed.
The captives were told to take the trail by which they had come.
Looking Glass shook hands with Frank Carpenter, but had no
conversation with him aside from telling him that they would
not be killed and would be permitted to return. White Bird did
not appear to the captives. He did not know a word of English,
and consequently kept away from them. The party on starting
away was told by Poker Joe that he could no longer control his
warriors.

The Captives Attacked.

The two parties then separated. Looking Glass and White
Bird, thinking everything was safe, started ahead of the Indian

camp. They did not know the little party was followed by the young warriors. On being informed that such was the case, they immediately sent Poker Joe to protect the whites. All this time the party were surrounded and followed by the most ferocious young men of the camp. Two of the white men left the camp and escaped into the brush. Mr. and Mrs. [George F.] Cowan were in advance of the rest of the party, when two Indians dashed down the hill in front of them. One of these Indians was Um-till-tilp-cown, one of the the three Idaho murderers. This Indian thought the murder of the whites an agreeable pastime, and he stepped forward and shot Cowan, who fell from his horse after being shot. Mrs. [Emma] Cowan immediately dismounted and endeavored to prevent the fiends, who had approached the wounded man, from doing him further injury, telling them to kill her but spare her husband. Her entreaties were unheeded, and she was torn from her husband, and he was shot through the head and left for dead.

While this fiendish work was being performed, another Indian came up. Seeing the women crying, and on learning the cause of their grief, he remembered Looking Glass' command to spare the lives of citizens. We remember asking this Indian why he interfered.

He replied: "I had not the heart to see those women abused. I thought we had done them enough wrong in killing their relations against the wishes of our chief, and knew we were in the wrong. While I was endeavoring to stop the bloody work, Poker Joe came up, having been sent by Looking Glass. He did not arrive in time to save those already shot, but he and I prevented other injuries being done the party."

When asked why it was that the life of Frank Carpenter had been spared, and being told that Carpenter attributed his being saved to the fact of his having made the sign of the cross, the same Indian said: "Oh! bosh; I am the man who saved his life, and interfered in his behalf for the reason I gave before, that I thought we had done enough killing. I took pity on the women, seeing their tears. I saw the man making the sign of the cross, but that had nothing to do with saving his life. I am down on preachers. They are the cause of most of these troubles. We are neither Catholics nor Protestants — we are infidels. I do not care to what denomination a preacher belongs. They preach for their own good, to fill their own pockets." The name of this Indian was Red Scout.

After the bloody work had been accomplished it was decided to take the women back to the camp. One of them was mounted behind Henry Lababour, the murderer of the men at Dearborn, Elk Creek and Rock Creek. This Indian was a Snake half-breed. The other lady was mounted behind Red Scout. Mrs. Cowan states that after being put behind an Indian on horseback she looked back and saw an Indian pounding her husband's head with a rock. The Indians deny this. They say the man was not touched after being shot. That they supposed him dead.

On again reaching the Nez Perces camp the captives were taken to Poker Joe's lodge. Poker Joe gave the warriors to understand that the women were under his protection and that he would permit no insult to be offered them. Poker Joe was the best friend the women had in the Nez Perces camp. The next day a council of the chiefs was held and Looking Glass said that the prisoners must be allowed to return. During the absence of the warriors Poker Joe took the two women and their brother some distance from the camp, and told them to make all possible haste if they wished to escape. His advice was followed and the party escaped.

The Helena Party — "Good Medicine for Sore Ears"

About the Helena party, the published account was strictly true. We endeavored to find from White Bird the name of the Indian who gave chase to the colored servant captured with this last party. A young warrior responded that he was the one who had been after the colored individual. [Ben] Stone managed to make his escape by climbing a tree. The Indian being interrogated as to why he wanted him so badly said: "I just wanted his scalp: colored men's hair is good medicine for sore ears." This accounts for the long chase given Stone.

The Nez Perces War of 1877, Continued.

When the Nez Perces were camped at Bear Paw Mountains Poker Joe grew dissatisfied with the other chiefs for not making their way into the British Possessions. Poker Joe had a good deal of influence over the Indians, but after a discussion with the chiefs, and they not agreeing to his plans, he declined having anything further to do with their future movements. Howard's whereabouts were known to the Indians. They knew his animals were worn out, while their own were in splendid condition. As a consequence they were in no hurry to move their camp, and spent their time in making merry, as they then had no doubt but they would effect their escape without difficulty. They had no intimation of the approach of the troops under Gen'l [Nelson A.] Miles.

The Bear Paw Battle.

While resting in fancied security on the morning of the attack, the scouts being all in camp, an alarm was suddenly given. The cry was "Prepare for a fight; there is a large body of soldiers close on us." White Bird ordered his warriors to prepare for a defense and said: "What a pity we did not have scouts out. Had we known this half an hour ago, how differently might we now have been situated. Had I known then of the approach of the soldiers we would not have to fight. Our horses are fresh and we could have made our escape. But it is too late now. Escape is impossible — fight we must."

About the battle of Bear Paw, I have not much to write, as the Indian version is but a repetition of the published accounts. The Indians got worsted in the engagement, as is well known and the white man's version was the true one. I purpose relating, however, the conversation between Looking Glass and White Bird; some facts in relation to the officer who was taken prisoner; and the promises made Joseph by the commanding officer in charge of the soldiers in case the Indians would surrender.

Gen'l Miles, like many others, supposed Joseph to be the leader of the hostiles, and wanted his surrender in place of the real leader — Looking Glass. This suited the Indians exactly and they

General Nelson A. Miles

Source: Library of Congress, Photograph Division, Washington, D.C.,
DIG-cwpb-06149.

allowed Joseph to go to the camp of the soldiers. That night he
remained in the tent of Gen'l Miles. During the truce the Indians
were engaged in fortifying their position, and some soldiers under command of Lieutenant Irvine who ventured into the Indian
camp were taken prisoners and held as a hostage for the return of
Joseph. The fight was renewed at this time. On the second day
in the afternoon an exchange was effected, the soldiers returning
to their command and Joseph to the Indian camp. Before the
exchange, while the fight was in progress, one of the warriors was
in need of some needle gun cartridges. He went to the officer
who was yet a prisoner and told him what he wanted. He asked
for two cartridges, and was given five by the officer, whose name
I was told was Lieut. Irvine. A few such men as him in the Indian
camp would have made more trouble for the soldiers.

Help Expected from Sitting Bull.

While the fight was in progress many of the Indian women
and a few children made their escape. A large part of the camp
believed that Sitting Bull was near at hand and that he would
come to their rescue. One of the women had escaped at the first
appearance of the soldiers and it was thought she had gone to the
Sioux camp. But such was not the case, as the woman went but a
short distance and remained until the fight was over.

Joseph Proposes to Surrender.

On the evening of the fourth day a flag of truce was raised
for the third time. Gen. Miles told the Indians that if they surrendered he would treat them well; that he would take them to
Tongue River that winter and in the spring would send them
back to Idaho. He furthermore said that any promises he might
make to them would be fulfilled. Joseph wanted to surrender
but the other chiefs kept him from doing so. They feared that in
case they were to surrender to Gen. Miles, they would be treated
similarly to the Indians who surrendered to Col. Wright on the
Columbia in 1858. After surrendering, the principals were all
hung by command of the officer to whom they surrendered. Joseph endeavored to persuade the chiefs that the best thing they

could do was to accede to the demands made by Gen. Miles. Looking Glass and White Bird then said: "Joseph, you do not know the Americans as well as we do. Never in the world will they fulfill the promises made the Indians. The commanding officer speaks sweet, but it is doubtful whether he will send the Indians back to their country." Next morning Joseph told Looking Glass he had concluded to surrender to Gen. Miles. The latter chief then went to White Bird, told him the conclusion arrived at by Joseph and said: "We will leave here tonight. I know we will never see our country again."

Death of Looking Glass and Poker Joe.

Near the Indian camp was a ridge on which some of the warriors lay watching the movements of the soldiers. Looking Glass, his brother and the other chiefs were in the camp talking over the proposed flight in the evening. Looking Glass requested his brother to get him his pipe, saying he wanted a smoke. While his brother had gone for the pipe Looking Glass had his attention attracted by the movement of the warriors on the ridge. He started towards them. He was asked to remain where he was, but the chief replied that he would return shortly; that he wanted to see what the warriors on the ridge were doing. He reached the place where the warriors were. It was some 500 or 600 yards from the soldiers' position. He raised himself up to view the surroundings. As he did so a volley from the guns of the soldiers was directed towards him, and one of the bullets entered his forehead, throwing him some distance down the hill and killing him instantly. Poker Joe, the friend of the lady prisoners taken in the National Park, was also killed in the Bear Paw fight.

The Escape.

White Bird and his warriors escaped that night. In the escaping party were 103 warriors, 60 women, 8 children and about 200 head of horses. One remarkable feature of the party was that there were no dogs with them. An Indian procession is usually considered incomplete unless there are in it a number of these latter animals. In a residence of thirty years in the Indian country I have not heard of a parallel case.

Joseph could have escaped as well as White Bird, but the conditions promised him by Gen'l Miles influenced him to surrender. If he had endeavored to escape, he would have had on his hands his wounded warriors and helpless women and children. He thought it the better plan to rely on the word of the officer to whom he surrendered — the representative of a nation of forty millions of people.

The Nez Perces War of 1877, Continued.
Meeting of the Chiefs White Bird and Sitting Bull.

After White Bird made his escape from the U.S. troops at Bear Paw and before he reached Sitting Bull's camp, he lost seven warriors by the Assiniboines and Gros Ventres. One of the killed was Umti-lilp-cown, the third and last of the Nez Perces who committed the murders in Idaho which brought on the war.

White Bird did not know whether or not it would be safe for him to go to Sitting Bull's camp, but after a consultation with his followers they came to the conclusion they might as well be killed by Indian enemies as by the whites. Coming to a half-breed camp near Milk River, they hired one of the party to guide them to Sitting Bull. As they were proceeding toward the Sioux camp they came upon an Indian skinning a buffalo. The hunter appeared rather shy, but after considerable parley told White Bird that he was a Sioux and that he had come from Sitting Bull's camp. White Bird told him to go to Sitting Bull and tell him the Nez Perces were anxious to see him; that they were refugees, fleeing for protection from the U.S. troops. The buffalo hunter started on his mission and the Nez Perces camp moved slowly in the direction he had gone. After marching a few miles they discovered a large body of mounted Indians coming toward them. They numbered nearly 3,000 warriors and were coming at full speed. A short distance in advance of the main body rode an Indian warrior, on a magnificent war horse. When within hailing distance of the Nez Perces the command halted. The warrior in advance asked White Bird, by signs, to what tribe he belonged.

White Bird made answer, saying he was a Nez Perces. The other then said: "I am Sitting Bull, and these," pointing to his followers, "are my warriors." Sitting Bull then came up and shook hands with White Bird and his warriors. After bidding them welcome, he said: "I am sorry indeed that your skin is like mine, that your hair is like mine, and that every one around you is a pure red man like myself. We, too, have lost our country by falsehood and theft."

Expecting an Attack.

Although the Indians were now north of the line, they expected to be followed and attacked by U.S. soldiers. The Sioux had not thus far been attacked, but they did not know but now that so many soldiers were near them they would follow the Indians and give them battle. Sitting Bull, after hearing of the Bear Paw fight, said: "If I had known you were surrounded by soldiers at Bear Paw Mountains, I certainly would have helped you. What a pity that I was not there with my warriors. But now you are here, and as long as you are with me I will not allow the Americans to take even a child from you without fighting for it." Sitting Bull received a present of seven horses from White Bird. The Nez Perces were welcomed in the Sioux camp and received from Sitting Bull nothing but the kindest of treatment.

The Nez Perces War of 1877, Continued.

While on my way from Fort Walsh to see the escaped Nez Perces, I was overtaken by Col. [Acheson G.] Irvine and command of the Mounted Police. The officer on learning my destination to be Sitting Bull's camp said he was also going there, his errand being to escort White Bird to Fort Walsh to have a talk with an American officer, Capt. [George W.] Baird by name. On the road Col. Irvine engaged me [to] act as interpreter for him. While looking for the Sioux camp we found a small party of Indians belonging to that camp and from them we learned that White Bird was with Crazy Horse's band of about 300 lodges at a place called Sandy Hills. In a short time we reached the camp and I never saw Indians so badly frightened as were these. We dismounted and Col. Irvine and your correspondent proceeded to White Bird's lodge. Arrived there we shook hands with the chief. His warriors thought we had come to arrest their chief — that we were hirelings of the U.S. Government — and they continued to arrive and crowd themselves into the lodge until we were packed so closely there was not room to move.

A Good Officer.

I never saw an officer with a better "Indian way" than Col. Irvine. He seemed to understand the Indian nature, and at once impressed the Indians favorably toward him.

We remained in the lodge but a short time. Then seeing the Indians were still somewhat uneasy we concluded we had best retire without mentioning at the present our mission to the chief.

White Bird Goes to Fort Walsh.

It will be remembered there were three Nez Perces sent direct from Fort Leavenworth. One of them was a brother-in-law of White Bird. The government thought best to send these men to White Bird, as they might possibly induce him to surrender. The emissaries were in company [of the] Police. It required considerable persuasion to induce the chief to accompany us to Fort Walsh. The Sioux told White Bird if he went with us to Fort Walsh he would be arrested. This had the effect of causing a delay of three days, but White Bird finally concluded to go with us and see the American officer. He was escorted by eight warriors only. On reaching the Fort Capt. Baird received the Nez Perces kindly, and they had no reason whatever to complain of their treatment.

The Council.

The morning after our arrival at the Fort we were called to the council, which was held in the officers' hall. Capt. Baird at once said to the chief: "An officer of the Queen wrote to the American authorities stating that the escaped Nez Perces were tired of their treatment by the British and wished to return to American soil. The officer to whom the complaint was made told them he would communicate with the American authorities and find out on what terms they would be allowed to return. The letter was received by the U.S. authorities and I was sent with these three members of your tribe to meet you and take you to Joseph. I want you to come with me. You will be treated well and taken down the river on a steamer." White Bird replied: "What are you going to do with Joseph? You hold him a prisoner of war. You promised to send him back to his country, but you have not done so. I want to know what you intend to do with him."

Capt. Baird then said: "Joseph is down at Leavenworth and expects to meet you. He wants you to come to him. If you accompany me to him it is likely you will be sent back to Idaho. If you do not come with me it is not likely Joseph will be returned to his country. I want you to take time to think. You can have a council among your people if you so desire."

Col. [James F.] Macleod then said to White Bird: "I have no doubt but that this man is telling you the truth, and that he firmly believes you will be treated as he says. You will be taken down to your own people. You will see Joseph. Your transportation will cost you nothing. Think well of these things. You have before you some of your people who come from Joseph, and that ought to satisfy you that the Nez Perces are treated well where they now are at Ft. Leavenworth."

All then left the room except the Nez Perces and the writer. White Bird then asked the Nez Perces from Ft. Leavenworth what Joseph had said. They replied: "Joseph told us to tell you that you might do as you thought best. If you conclude to go to him he will be glad to see you — if not, well and good."

White Bird said: "Well, there is a mistake somewhere. The officer tells me Joseph expects me to go to him. If you have told me the truth then this man has told me what is false." That ended the first day's council.

At the Second Council,

Capt. Baird but repeated what he had before said, and added: "You may possibly imagine that you may return, one by one, to Idaho from this place, and be safe in doing so. But you are mistaken in this, and should you attempt it [you] will be arrested. If you return with me you will have no trouble whatever.

White Bird (left)
No Hunter, brother of Looking Glass (right)

Source: Glenbow Archives, Calgary, Alberta, Canada, NA-5501-8.

I come for you on the representations made by the officers of the Queen that you and your people had tired of your home and desired to return."

White Bird asked: "Am I the man, or has any of the leading men of my tribe expressed themselves as wanting to return with you? I do not want to go where Joseph is. The country is unhealthy. Let Joseph come back here, and together we will return to Idaho of our own accord."

Colonel Macleod again said, "I have no doubt this man is telling you the truth. May be you think there are plenty of buffalo and you can depend on these animals for food. We have so many Indians here the buffalo will not last long. You have no right to this country. We can make no treaties with you. I can give nothing save my protection. You had better retire to your lodge and think over this matter. You must not think only for yourself, but for your people — warriors, women and children — and not for one or two days, but for years to come."

It is not remembered whether it was before or after this speech of Col. Macleod that Yellow Bull said: "While we were engaged in the battle at Bear Paw Mountains the chief of the soldiers said if we surrendered we would be sent back to our country and treated well." The Preacher, or Bald Head, and the third Indian repeated the remarks made by Yellow Bull.

White Bird then resolved that he would not accompany Capt. Baird. He thought the soldiers had told him falsehoods regarding the country and climate to which they would be taken. The Nez Perces tribe had already met with large losses. He could not see the necessity of going to Fort Leavenworth and thence to Idaho. It was a shorter journey from where he was than from Fort Leavenworth, and he will wait until the return of Joseph before leaving the British possessions.

The party making the complaint which led to this council was Henry Tavahvour, the leading murderer in the band of Nez Perces which passed through Montana last year. He and his companions deserted from White Bird's camp.

White Bird refuses to surrender unless Joseph returns, but does not intend to again war against the whites.

White Bird and Sitting Bull.
The Conference of the Chiefs and White Bird's Relation of the Conversation.
No Probability of an Early Outbreak — What the Nez Perces Want and Where the Danger Lies.

In compliance with your request to put you in possession of my views concerning the probability of an outbreak on the part of the Indians of the Northwest, I may as well state at once that I am firmly convinced there is not the slightest chance of one for the present. Of course this opinion has no reference to the possibility of isolated crimes, even as the general peace of the State prevents not occasional Klu Klux raids. Others will more ready understand this conclusion by a perusal of one of my conversations with White Bird, which is hereto appended.

White Bird said: "Among other councils which I have had with Sitting Bull there was one in which he strongly advised me to prevent my Indians from crossing the line, saying: 'We must do as the Police tell us — behave ourselves here and not go or allow our men to go into American (U.S. of course) Possessions to commit depredations. Should we do so, we will surely get into trouble. The Police don't lie like the Americans, and we must respect them. Now mind what I say, we get our protection from them, and we must respect our protectors!' To this I quite agreed, adding, however, that some of my Indians are deserting me; they do so when I am sound asleep in my bed; they run off at night, and if these men commit depredations I am not to blame. You know that I am doing my best to keep them here. I don't want to fight any more. When the fighting was commenced in Idaho it was brought on and continued to be forced upon me, independent of wish or action of mine. After it had begun I only wished to lead my people to the Buffalo country, and in doing so was again and again forced into battle. Now, I came over here simply as to an asylum, and and am waiting Joseph's return to Idaho. He was promised by General Miles that if he surrendered he would be taken back there. Joseph could have escaped as well as myself but the condition of the surrender was good; but, although I have since heard that otherwise Joseph was well treated by the General, that promise was a lie. I was glad when we quit fighting, and here I am with my warriors awaiting news from Joseph. If the government sends him back to his home in Idaho I will at once go back and make peace. In fact, we have always wanted peace, but by the action first of individual White men and Red men it has been denied us, and then when soldiers charged on us we were compelled to fight. If Joseph is moved to the Indian Territory I will not surrender, because it is against my will and Joseph's will to go to that place. The United States recognizes Indians as nations and not as slaves. Why does she want to coop us up in a bad climate that will cause us to die in a short time? Is it right for the American government, after fighting a nation and defeating it, to imprison it in a place where it must quickly perish? Is it right for a strong man if he finds a horse in the possession of a weak one and makes an offer therefor, which the owner declines, to take the horse away, and, in the case of poor resistance being made, to abuse that weak man even unto death? We were here before the white men knew there was such a country. I don't want to fight, I want justice from the Americans, and if I cannot get it I am going to remain in the North and do the best I can for subsistence.

"No doubt that for many years, or so long as Joseph remains in Indian Territory, I in the British Possessions and the remainder of the Nez Perces in Idaho, many men are liable to be murdered. As soon as Joseph reaches Indian Territory his men will start, at night if need be, for their old homes. My Indians do the same thing, and others in Idaho will travel to see their countrymen now with Joseph or myself. Many of these are men who have seen their mothers and sisters, wives and children all destroyed and there is nothing to restrain them. They would as soon be killed as kill, and sooner kill a white man than not, caring nothing as to what is left behind or who suffers. It would be best for all if the Government would get these Indians together.

"I hear that the Government is very anxious about reducing the number of its soldiers in order to save expenses. I suppose some men want to steal the money for some other purpose and leave the settlers and Indians to murder one another. But if they really want to be economical why don't they fulfill their treaties? Then there would be no trouble. I have seen enough. We can all see how the Red Coat Government treats its Indians. It has jurisdiction over the Indians for any kind of crime. The American Government has not, because, I presume, it would require too much expense. But which spends the most money? I know little of these matters, but I see a Police force of 300 men controlling 25,000 or 30,000 Indians — some of the worst in America — when the United States cannot do it with thousands of soldiers."

[Duncan:] I may here add a remark which I hope those who take the trouble to read these papers will bear in mind, applicable throughout. Objections may be found to my translations of Indian speeches, etc., the objectors no doubt supposing that words and phrases used are foreign to Indian thought. To such I can only give an assurance that in every instance my aim is and shall be to convey as correct an expression as I am capable of giving of the speech or conversation translated. Be it known, however, that my command of the English language is by no means adequate to give a fair idea of the capacity of even a moderate Indian speaker. There are, I believe, few white men who, in variety of expression, vividness of description, intonation, or even grace of action, surpass the first-class orators of the Red Men, and in this belief I have no doubt I will be joined by white men who in this matter have the means and power of judging.

Appendix 1:
Supplemental Essays

Indian Feeling.
An Interesting Exposition of the Indian Side of the Case.
by Duncan McDonald
[From *The New North-West* (Deer Lodge, Mont.), June 14, 1878, p. 3, c. 5-6.]

"Red Mountain" said on hearing of the further removal of his people with Joseph:

"The President of the Americans could protect Joseph and my people if they were brought back to my counry. He does not wish to do it. He does not wish to satisfy the Indians. He will not. Now, my people are removed to a country further away and a country not so healthy. What are his intentions? What is he doing. He excites them more. The people on these waters will feel it. The President heeds not the cause. The more trouble we make the better is his purpose advanced, as the more we war the sooner we will be destroyed. Is it not before you — sorrow and blood and exile and weeping? But he cares not. I am glad there were a few men in his house who are our friends; but he did not heed what they said. He gave his consent to the men who were not our friends — yes, to men who sent my people and Joseph away. Is he a wolf? The big white buffalo wolf is kind to the little red coyotes, but our great White Chief sends our little ones out of the way. Does he want us to make war again? He always said 'Stop! Stop!'"

Not Beaten, But Betrayed.

In that you will see some of the truth. All the fighting of last year did not displace the idea my people of the West had in their heads. They have no idea that they were beaten. They say the red man helped the white man to beat them and it can be proven; that it was not the armies of Generals Howard and Gibbon and Terry and Miles alone that conquered that little band of the Nez Perces. It is known that it was done in a great measure by Indian help.

Strength of the Hostiles.

At the present day, on a close computation, there are above the Cascade Ridge on the Columbia's waters, on this side of the boundry line of America and British America, about thirty-two hundred men of arms, and if well mounted and determined on a decided combination they could remove their families to distant countries and fight to the bitter end for loss of human rights. Twenty-five hundred of them are equally brave with the Nez Perces and in such unlucky event it would take ten times their number five years to tell a desolated country that the living could sleep well in it. The proper way of dealing with the red man and of teaching him how the white man has acquired his present estate has never, that I have seen, been advanced. Men and papers give various views, but the stream passes on and the red man is being destroyed.

The Difference of Creeds.

The white man rants and warbles of civilization and religion. What is civilization? What is religion? The Churches' hymn about a Christ. Has not the first sound of that name been his ruin? What did it bring to the red man? The experience of 400 years proves to him that which his evil genius foretold is now confirmed and has been at his own door. Even men who in their own countries cowered before their fellow man like squirrels before a hound come forth and scream, "Gather them on Reservations." "Take the reservations." "Clean the d—d Indians all out." And as if to satisfy and maintain the serpent in their wills you open the Statute Book of this beautiful Territory and read these damning words to be found on page 178, section 13, of the Criminal Practice Act:

"No black or mulatto person or Indian or Chinese shall be permitted to give evidence in favor of or against any white person. Every person who shall have one-eighth part or more of negro blood shall be deemed a mulatto; and every person who shall have one-half of Indian blood shall be deemed an Indian."

[In this our correspondent has fallen into error. He quotes from the "Bannack Statutes" of 1864. The Criminal Practice Act adopted in the codification of 1872, in accordance with the laws of Congress, contains no such provision, and an Indian or Chinese or Negro of any degree of blood is now a competent witness in any court of law in this or any Territory or State in the Union. But when as intelligent and educated a man as our correspondent holds so erronious a view of existing laws, it is fair to presume the Nez Perces and other Indians all so understand it, and the Statute is to them as if it still stood on the books. — Ed. N. N. W.]

In a country which holds these horrible sentiments true civilization and what is worth anything of that much prostituted term Christianity, are of non-effect. Talk about Indian Rings, Agents, Missionaries, Government and Armies: this sentiment on your statute books is the real poison in the blood of the people of the United States.

Fruit From the Seed.

The first grim confirmation the Columbia Indians had of it was the refusal to take any measures to punish the cold-blooded murder of Elijah, the young and popular Chief of the Walla Wallas before the white man massacre took place. Since then repeated murders followed. The white man tried to evade them — would not give ear to the red men who kept a strict account of them year by year in their minds. The more the years passed on the more the criminal numbers grew, and the sense of hatred to the white man grew with them.

In 1855 the Indians were told on the treaty grounds that "If they did not sell their lands they would be taken from them." These words were never forgotten. They were the chief arrows in the quiver of Kayuse war of that year. It was all compulsion, and the author of them, with his friends, would not have lived to repeat them had the Nez Perces yielded to the proposition of striking him then and there. But the kind, brave and unscrupulous [Governor Isaac I.] Stevens met a braver death years afterward in the battles of his own people.

Aggravating Circumstances.

With the steadily increasing pressure and unredressed crimes of the white men in their country and with the presence of Howard to remove them from their long-loved homes — homes of which they never relinquished title even were they disposed to leave them, and with their Speaker seized at the point of the bayonet for representing these truths and others of secondary force the Nez Perces determined to revenge their long pent grievances in the terrible way they did. In Indian laws an armed man putting his hand on man is punishable with death. When these Indians, before the time I was born, were in their prime it was death for one Indian to strike another, as it was also for adultery, or in defense of any seizure of property from its proper owner.

Nomadic Life.

Having made these few most serious observations, I have a little to say on the cry against nomad life. It is wrong for you to think my people are bad because they lead a nomadic life. Where is there a more nomadic tribe than the Flatheads? Yet in the day of need you cried to them for help, and they helped you as far as human nature could do, although they love you fully as little as the Nez Perces. Every Indian's country is his ranche where he has fixed fisheries and little humble huts and fields and marsh ground for his roots and cereals and higher bowers for his fruits. There are left with them a few brood horses or cows in charge of the aged or laborers and the adventurous ones go to secure more comfort and game and trade, as your ships go to the seas for oils and to Canton and the other far off countries for teas and silks. And, withal, egress and return wear off grievances, local animosities are assuaged and happier life is secured. Were it not for the trips "to Buffalo," it is probable that the Nez Perces war had been of earlier date and a much bloodier one. The great war chiefs of the West, Aeneas, Jutraikan and others, never went to Buffalo nor one in a hundred of their people, and I learn that the monsters of New York and Paris and London and the Bender family never ran buffalo at all. The white man may shift the causes as he pleases flattering his one-sided, crucifying and crucified Christianity, but the design, the determination, the fang, the aspiration, *the continent* are in his own head. Look at the text of it from his own words: "If you do not give your land it will be taken from you, and if a white man kill you none of you can witness in my courts against him." The Irishman may curse the Englishman, the Jew the Roman, the Roman the Goth and the Turk the Russian, but such a sentence as the above was never in prospective or real cruelty surpassed. Does not every tree produce his own seed?

Hostile Religions.

Again, we see it advocated through the public papers to open the reservations! A most fallacious suggestion. If a farmer has his rails, the reservation lines are the Indian's fence. What we do want is ampler reservations and true knowledge and thrift and expansion of our little inventive powers; material aid given for material wealth and a great country taken from us; true sympathy and cheer instilled and just freedom to go and come as you would have yourself. But the mere story that a snake spoke to a woman somewhere; that a medicine man went up a mountain somewhere; that a big chief was with his soldiers drowned somewhere; that a young brave killed a big man with a stone; that a married maid had a child in a stable; that he took all the people from hell; that there are plenty in hell yet — these old sayings are of little avail to the Red man. He has many such pages himself. But I am not going to startle you with a recital of them at present. Otherwise I might say that some tall Red Man saw these plains from the beginning and tell you how one of Montana's ancient ancestors laid his hand on the noonday sun and put his left elbow on the steep of the cold grizzly bear long, long ago.

The Nez Perces' Resolve.

Coming to our own times, however, and to stern reality, you may like to hear the last words of the Nez Perces when their resolve had been taken an the burning expressions on their brains hung smothered on their lips. They said:

"It is thus done. This is our dust. Here is our home. The white man takes it from us. Who took it shall not keep it. He will enter the earth with us. Those who come after them will take it and will not be disturbed."

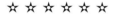

Goaded to the War-Path.
The Circumstances That Incited Wallitze to Commence the Nez Perces War.

[From *The New North-West* (Deer Lodge, Mont.), June 21, 1878, p. 3, c. 4]

The name of Wallitze was mentioned in earlier papers as one of the three men who inaugurated the Nez Perces war in 1877. His father had been killed by a white man. The following memoranda furnished by Mr. McDonald will be of interest in showing from what trivial circumstances the assault upon the whites near Mount Idaho originated:

I insert here some account of Wallitze during the few days before he commenced his bloody work. Wallitze was a fine-looking Indian and the Nez Perces had laws something like the Turks — one might have as many wives as he chose. Wallitze was a gay Lothario among his tribe, and one evening he made love to one of the red female beauties, and advancing toward her asked her to go with him to his lodge. At his request she consented and went with him. Early the next morning the mother of the girl was told her daughter had gone to live with Wallitze. She started for his lodge raving mad, entered the lodge and seeing her daughter lying with Wallitze she took hold of the girl and threw her toward the door. Then turning to Wallitze she said: "You, Wallitze, have had many wives and fine women, but you have no regard for them. You always leave them. You neither love nor support any of them. I do not want my daughter treated in that manner. I see you are a man who likes to go after women and try and insult our people. But you did not act like a man when your father Tip-iala-natzilkan was murdered. There he lies in his grave a little way off, and here you are. Why don't you go after the whites?"

To these words Wallitze gave no notice. That evening there was a Kissing Dance among the Nez Perces, a place where many an Indian would have been pleased if Wallitze had not gone. On reaching the dancing floor and while dancing around he was told by one of the young braves, a relative of the girl he took the night before: "Here you are again. You need not be so stylish when in public. We know you are a coward." Of these words he took no notice. On the second round the language was repeated by the same Indian. Wallitze stopped and asked, "Do you mean what you say?" The brave replied, "I do. You are a coward and nothing else. There is your father's grave. He was murdered by a white man and you have not the manliness to kill him who slew your father." Wallitze being thus spoken to in the presence of so many women and men of his own people was abashed. "All right," he said, "you will be sorry for what you have spoken." He left the dance and went to his lodge to sleep. The next morning at daybreak he was up. Some Indians say that Tip-sis-ill-pilp was with him already, but the third man, the young boy, was not seen. He said: "I remember the last words of my father. He said, tell Wallitze, my son, for my sake and for the sake of his brothers and sisters and for all the Nez Perces nation to hold his temper and not let his desire for revenge get the best of him. We are a nation poor in property; in fact, we have nothing. The white man has plenty of all things and we have nothing. We can make neither guns nor ammunition. We love our country, and above all our families. Do not go to war. You will lose your country, and still greater will be the loss of life. This was his message to me. But now I am going to satisfy the man who insulted me last night." On this very day Wallitze, Tap-sis-ill-pilp and the third, whose name I cannot learn, began their bloody work on the Idaho settlements.

D. M.

Both Wallitze and Tap-sis-ill-pilp were killed in the battle of the Big Hole.

An Appeal to Reason.
The Injustice and Folly of Threatening All Indians With Death Because Some Are Murders.
by Duncan M'Donald
[From *The New North-West* (Deer Lodge, Mont.), Aug. 16, 1878, p. 3, c. 4.]

On my return from the British Possessions I was very much annoyed and grieved to learn of the murders recently committed by a returning band of the Nez Perces. I also read two letters in your issue of the 19th ult. from your correspondents at Philipsburg, referring to the same subject, and thought in connection with these papers a few remarks thereupon would not be inappropriate. Knowing, however, that many unreasoning men would receive any adverse criticism from me merely as a proof of my sympathy with the murderers, and that many others, with more brains but still with strong prejudices, would take advantage of the general indignation at the crimes to favor the same view, I deferred any remarks I felt inclined to make until the natural excitement of the time should be somewhat allayed. Having now learned that the majority of the criminals have met with just punishment in the shape of death and wounds, I feel it is only those whose opinions are not worthy of consideration who will blame me for pointing out wherein such letters as those referred to are fraught with general injury. Unfortunately my *New North-West* of the 19th has been destroyed, and I am, therefore, unable to take *seriatim* exceptions. However, there are four points I wish to make and these are:

First — It is entirely wrong, unreasonable and unjust to support the idea that it is right or advisable to kill all Indians because you do not know which are hostile and which are not. To argue on such an apparent truism would, no doubt, seem a waste of words; but, unhappily, there are others that well know there exists a type of humanity that would readily send a bullet through a defenseless Indian or white man solely for the purpose of acquiring the character of a big brave, and that the only restraint on such is the sentiment of decent society and a wholesome fear of the law. Some men are, of course, to a great extent irrational. I cannot believe that men of the evident intelligence of your correspondents belong to such a category, but presume that their feelings on hearing of the deaths of their neighbors overcame their powers of reason. Their opinions, however, published in a respectable journal, by encouraging the class above referred to, are capable of much greater evils than any individual action, not to mention the absurdity of urging the propriety of killing the first Frenchman met because another had murdered some one — they actually appear to approve of the principle of killing a Frenchman on account of a murder by an Italian. Do they not know that two Indian nations are as separate and distinct as any two nations of Europe? Their customs, languages, modes of living and very often their food and methods of transportation are totally dissimilar. Why a Flathead who last year proved his friendship for, or, if some prefer it, his disinclination to hostility toward the whites, should be subject to be shot by the first white man who has a safe opportunity simply because said white man does not know he is not a hostile Nez Perce passes comprehension. Of course no man, no matter to what extent he may be accused of a sentiment or other sympathy with the Red Man, is prepared to deny the fact that "The Progress of Civilization," "Survival of the Fittest," "Struggle for Existence" — no matter by what term we recognize the decree of Fate — has rendered inevitable the final extinction of Indians, but neither the sentiment of the civilized world nor the philanthropy of Americans is likely to hasten the fulfillment of that decree by sanctioning a general holocaust.

But, secondly, apart from a want of reason in support of their views, and there are very strong ones in opposition thereto, everyone must know that if a few, or even one Flathead, Pen d'Oreille or Spokane Indian was killed for no better reason than that proposed by one of your correspondents, a general uprising of Montana Indians would almost inevitably take place, and before their annihilation was effected (supposing that to be the consummation aimed at) many valuable lives and much treasure would necessarily be expended, although Philipsburg might not be immediately affected.

And here comes the most reprehensible portion of the correspondence, in which one of the writers remarks upon their being "plenty of men at that place." It will probably strike others as it did me that were he alone or with a family on one of the outlying farms of Montana he might not be quite so ready to stir up an Indian war. On the contrary I fancy he would have no very friendly feelings towards the man who, backed by hundreds of strong arms, exhibited his courage by provoking the massacre of defenseless families.

Thirdly — A demand was made for the withdrawal of the regular army in order to make way for an extinction of the Indians. Now, with the writer's views the demand is certainly a most reasonable one, for the army is, without doubt, the Indians' best friend. As General [William] Sherman recently and nobly said, "The highest duty of an army is to make war upon war," and there can hardly be any doubt that had the U.S. forces been sufficient to prevent the citizens of the United States from making war on the Indians and the Indians from making war on the citizens, occasions for the army fighting Indians would have been few and far between. Nevertheless, had your correspondent his desire I think he would very soon discover that, were all the citizens of a country required to become fighting men for even the short period required to annihilate the Indians, said country would present a very unprosperous appearance long before the end had been attained.

Fourthly — Your correspondence contains a sneer at the Indian Agent of the Flatheads and other tribes. This, of course, Mr. [Peter] Ronan can well submit to, as it proves that he has moved out of the common rut, and it is always a consolation to be thought original. Who ever before heard of an Indian agent being accused of petting his charge? Wouldn't it astonish the Indian Department at Washington, though, to have, among the many complaints, one charging an agent with being too good to the Indians?

Seriously, does it not seem, that an agent who treats the Indians in such a manner as to impress them with some faith in the good intentions of the government and so prevent them from doing evil deserves commendation rather than otherwise? Of course I may be met with the statement that one of Agent Ronan's wards stole a bottle of whiskey and another a horse, to which I can only reply by asking if there is never a bottle or bill missed in Deer Lodge or Philipsburg the loss of which cannot be traced to a Red Man?

"Friendlies" or "Hostiles."
Mr. McDonald Excepts to Our Views of Indian Matters.
[From *The New North-West* (Deer Lodge, Mont.), Aug. 30, 1878, p. 3, c. 5.]
Editor New North-West.

In your notice of my last communication you have fallen into a few errors which, I think, if you desire to give a fair resume of the Indian situation you will consider it expedient to correct. These errors are less excusable than those of your Philipsburg correspondents as theirs are founded on their natural feelings and could be judged accordingly, while yours are based upon statements, made as facts, and therefore more calculated to lead reasoning people into error. You say that no Indians have a right to be away from their reservations, except when convoyed by soldiers, &c., &c. The *fact* is the treaty made with Indians of this reservation distinctly recognizes their right to visit the buffalo country, and as there is no proviso made as to their being accompanied by soldiers, the fact of the Government not being prepared to furnish a convoy by no means abrogates such right. Again you say that at the time of publication of aforesaid correspondence there were none of these Indians wandering about. To this I can only reply that there were Indians outside of the reservation on the Blackfoot, &c., &c., that the Flathead chief, Arlee, with a following was then en route from a buffalo hunt and might easily have chosen a path that would have brought him into contact with men imbued with the sentiments objected to. As to your elaborate argument in reference to rights of blockade, did it not strike you that even where the right safely existed that a certain amount of forewarning was given, while in the case in point, as the Flatheads, etc., have the misfortune not to be able to study the *New North-West,* (which I know many of them much regret) they would be very unlikely to be informed of their threatened death, and why they could expect no other treatment, as you assert, men who had but lately offered to furnish scouts to warn settlers of any approach of hostiles, seems rather difficult of explanation.

Could I examine your issue of the 19th ult., I still think I could find a sentence therein upon which I founded the statement that *one* of your correspondents wrote of the number of men, &c. Perhaps, however, I was entirely wrong; certainly, if I used quotation marks as printed, I made a great mistake, as I was, as acknowledged, writing from memory.

With reference to your not knowing instances of Indians being killed on account of the misdeeds of their brethren. I will remark that I could cover more space of your valuable sheet than you would be willing to allow with examples thereof; aye, and give witnesses, at present living in the Territory, in proof thereof. Mr. J. H. Robertson of your place could give you one very glaring case which occurred in Kootenai during his residence there.

Duncan McDonald

More About Indian "Medicine."
Recollections of the Author of the Nez Perces Papers.
[From *The New North-West* (Deer Lodge, Mont.), Feb. 21, 1879, p. 3, c. 3.]

Some two or three weeks ago we stated the author of the Nez Perces Papers did not believe in Indian "medicine." Since then we are in receipt of the following personal letter which we take the liberty of publishing:

"I again repeat my disbelief in Indian medicine. I have said the Indians get vexed with me on account of my disbelief, and although oftentimes placed in embarrassing positions on this account, I remain to this day unconverted.

"I was once with a war party of Pen d'Oreille Indians who had their horses stolen by the Blackfeet. We followed on foot in the hope that we might be able to get back the stolen animals. We started from the Marias River for the south fork of the Saskatchawan [sic] early in February. At night we were all completely worn out. After traveling several days without recovering out stock, we concluded to rest awhile and went into camp. That night I was very tired and slept soundly. On waking up in the morning, I observed one of the warriors painted and who shortly commenced singing his medicine song. He told us if we did as he said we would thereby save the life of one of our warriors. If not, the enemy (the Blackfeet) would take his life. We had had very cold weather, but the medicine of the painted warrior seemed to infuse new life and vigor into the others, and their actions to me were highly amusing. The medicine man said he wanted all the others to paint themselves. If any refused, the life of one of the warriors would be taken. At the same time he told us there was a Blackfoot Indian a few miles behind us and if we wanted his scalp we could go and get it without endangering ourselves. I told the warriors I did not believe the medicine man and would go on no wild goose chase.

"In obedience to the medicine man's command all the Indians painted themselves. Please bear in mind that the Pen d'Oreilles are called civilized Indians and good Christians. At this time a man named Linlay and myself were seated off to one side trying to avoid the painting process. We were forced to submit to it, however, and the scene was ludicrous in the extreme. Before singing our "medicine song," we had to say our prayers — the Lord's Prayer and three Hail Mary's. This latter we had to repeat with the regularity of clock work. Morning, noon and night we were obliged to say these prayers. At the same time we were after the scalps of the Blackfeet and wanted to make a raid on their horses. The Pen d'Oreilles say that unless a man is baptized by the Jesuites his soul is forever lost. We were told on this occasion that we could take the lives of our enemies and receive no punishment for so doing in the hereafter. In this connection I wish to say that Michael, the Pen d'Oreille chief, punishes severely to this day any member of his tribe who refuses to believe in his creed.

"One day during this trip, while we were camped on the Marias, I accompanied a hunting party. I killed two buffalo, but took only their tongues. We returned to the camp late in the evening, and brought down the wrath of the women on our heads for bringing no meat to camp. Chief Michael was engaged when we returned in making medicine to bring the herd of buffalo near the camp. Buffalo were scarce and Michael desired meat for the camp. In the night we were summoned by the chief to be present at his lodge while he made his medicine. Arrived there we found him divested of all clothing except a covering around his loins, painted from head to foot a bright red and standing in the centre of the lodge singing. He would sing a few minutes, and then assume an attitude to listen for the approach of the herd. He shortly announced the coming of the buffalo, but it is needless to say there was no truth whatever in his assertion.

"All this time there were millions of buffalo twenty miles from where the starving Indians were camped, but so great was their faith in the medicine of their chief that the poor, deluded followers, instead of going to the buffalo, relied wholly upon Chief Michael to bring the herd to them.

"Yes, I am a disbeliever, and what intelligent person would not be?

"Your truly,
"Duncan McDonald."

Appendix 2:
Letters From the North Country

Letters From Duncan McDonald.
His Visit to White Bird's Camp.
Some Interesting Items Apropos to the Present Indian
Troubles.

[From *The New North-West* (Deer Lodge, Mont.), July 26, 1878, p. 2, c. 4.]

Special Correspondence *New North-West.*

[We received on Monday evening, via Fort Benton, three letters from our correspondent, Mr. McDonald, dated at White Bird's Camp, British America July 2d. and Ft. Walsh, B. A., July 9th and 10th; also, on Tuesday morning, a letter from him at Missoula dated July 22d, he having reached Jocko on his return on the 20th. A portion of these letters were personal to the editor. We therefore extract from them such matters as are of general interest.—Ed. N. N. W.]

White Bird Does Not Wish to Surrender.

Fort Walsh, B. A.
July 2, 1878.

I have just returned from the Sioux camp. I was with Major [Acheson G.] Irvine, of the Mounted Police. He went to the Sioux camp for the purpose of bringing White Bird to Captain [George W.] Baird, one of the American officers. Capt. Baird is from Tongue River. White Bird does not wish to surrender just now. I will return home by way of Deer Lodge and will explain it when I see you.

Yours truly,
D. McDonald.

* * * * *

Frank Carpenter's Confounding of Persons.

White Bird's Lodge
British America,
July 9, 1878.

I have just received your letter inclosing Frank D. Carpenter's letter in relation to Poker Joe, Joe Hill, and White Bird being the same person; also as to his saving his life by making the sign of the cross. It seems he is rather sore at my discrediting his having saved his life by that sign. His ideas of the Christian Trinity are that the Father, the Son, and the Holy Ghost are one person; but White Bird is not the Father, nor Poker Joe the Son, nor Henry (Joe Hill) the Holy Ghost. I do not ask Mr. Carpenter for any favors. I am here in Crazy Horse's and the Nez Perces camp to find out all the facts of that campaign and they will appear in the *New North-West*. It would have surprised me more if Mr. Carpenter had credited me for what I have said about him. One of the main reasons of my coming to this camp is to find out whether Mr. Carpenter's story is reliable or not.

Poker Joe fought bravely and was killed in the fight in Bear Paw Mountains. White Bird is here and has been a kind man to me. Henry has gone across the mountains toward the Kootenai. If Mr. Carpenter is able to "bunch" these three men he must be possessed of Infinite Power. He ought to be ashamed of himself if he cannot write a more reliable story of those blood thirsty devils we call "the Indians." I had a long talk with the man who saved the Carpenter girls and their brother, Frank D. Carpenter.

Yours truly,
Duncan McDonald.

Fort Walsh, July 10 — I wrote you I would return by way of Deer Lodge, but I am sorry to inform you that my horses are worn out and I will be unable to go around that way. I will start for home to-morrow. I will write up the Nez Perces campaign on

my return and also advise you about the councils between Sitting
Bull and White Bird. * * * * *

D. M.

* * * * *

Some Light on Hitherto Mysterious Matters —
Nez Perces That Have Left White Bird.

Missoula, M. T., July 22, 1878.

I wrote you from Fort Walsh that I would return home
by way of Deer Lodge, but I failed. My horses were too nearly
worn out. I started from Fort Walsh on the 9th inst. and arrived at home on the 20th. I left White Bird at Sandy Hills,
about seventy miles north of Fort Walsh. I left his camp July 7th.
he has sixty-five warriors, about forty-five women, and about a
half dozen children. He is with Crazy Horse's band, consisting
of about 300 lodges. The oldest man in the Nez Perces camp is
White Bird. He is fifty years old, but looks rather young for his
age. I was with him for ten days.

There was a party of Nez Perces — about twenty altogether
— half of them women (Chief Joseph's daughter, a fine looking
girl of 16 or 17 among them) — deserted White Bird's camp
in the middle of the night and started for Idaho. It must have
been about the first of June when they left. Some of them told
the Indians remaining north that they were going to try to cross
the Kootenai pass if they could find the trail. On arriving at the
Dearborn I learned the Nez Perces were murdering men, and I
think they are the same party that left White Bird's camp on or
about the 1st of June. One of them is a half-breed who speaks
English. His name is Henry. He is the lad who got one of the
Carpenter girls to ride behind him on his horse in the National
Park last year.

I also saw the men who stole the horses on Sun river. They
were the same men who stole Gillette's watch, etc. There were
four of them. It was one of those men who saved the Carpenter
girls and their brother.

About a week before the twenty above mentioned left
White Bird's camp, Eagle of the Light's brother left. Joe Hill

left with him. There were three men and two or three women in the party. I think they are around Tobacco Plains, Kootenai — north of the line. Some time in June, after the twenty left another small party deserted — four or five men and the same number of women and children. The day after I arrived at Fort Walsh, the well known scout Captain John, son-in-law, and wife and child, started for Idaho. I met them at Fort Walsh. This is all the information I have of Nez Perces moving this way.

Referring again to Mr. Carpenter's letter, you can do as you please about publishing my answer, but Mr. C. is certainly wrong about those men. Joe Hale (Hill) is the man who started towards Kootenai. He is a brother of John Hill, the prisoner who was confined at the Missoula Post. Poker Joe was killed at Bear Paw mountains, and White Bird is at Sandy Hills.

Speaking again of the four thieves I have mentioned, one of them is a tall, good looking Indian, and is the one who saved the Carpenters, and is the man who rode with the other Carpenter girl. [Presumably, Mrs. [George F.] Cowan. — Ed. N. N. W.] His name is Red Scout.

My memoranda and papers in confusion yet. It will take me a week or two to get them in order. * * * * I had a long and tiresome trip, much of the time having no water to drink, except that found in little ponds.

Your truly,
Duncan McDonald

From Over the Line.
A Prospecting Party Falls in With a Band of the Hostile Nez Perces.
[From *The New North-West* (Deer Lodge, Mont.), Oct. 24, 1879, p. 2, c. 5-6.]

Old Hudson Bay Post, Oct. 5, 1879
Editor New North-West:

I received your letter on my return from the British Possessions, where a party of us went prospecting for but failed to find a fortune. The party consisted of three persons — Messers. Baird, Milton and myself. On our travels we reached

Tobacco Plains

where we found some Nez Perces belonging to White Bird's band. There were eleven lodges of them under Took-alex-see-ma, a brother of Looking Glass. The Indians want to consider him as their chief but he would not accept the offer, not wishing to be a leader of that camp. When we arrived, and before dismounting, we were approached by a number of them who extended their hands toward the expected "Boston men." Their women rushed away to the timber and brought us some firewood on their backs while we big, stout men were lying down smoking our pipes. These Indians are poor but not suffering from starvation. They brought us berries and cooked fish, and meat as gifts, not expecting anything in return. One woman brought us the last flour she had and offered it to "the Americans," but we thanked her and told her we had plenty.

The Nez Perces Case.

While camped with them Mr. Baird left us and started for the Kootenai mines to attend to business for T. J. Demers, while we remained in camp until two more "Boston men" arrived — one Mr. Hibern, and the other Mr. Ben. Welch, a brother of Mr. Dan. J. Welch of Missoula. They at first thought it a Kootenai camp until I told them the Indians were Nez Perces, at which they at first manifested some uneasiness, until I told them there was no danger — that these men had often said to me, "If Uncle Sam is so anxious for us to surrender we are willing to surrender to a boy if it would do any good. We would send what few guns we have to the United States Government if that would do any good. But, no! not satisfied to receive our guns, they must send us to the hot climate in the Indian Territory. We are willing to do anything the Government asks of us only to go to the Indian Territory where we will perish of fevers. We are dying fast enough without the great Government trying to make us die faster by sending us to a country where the climate is bad for us. We know these things. We get letters from Joseph's band and they tell us who dies. By the deaths we can tell they are dying very fast. We are willing to go to any reserve in Montana and Washington but that is not allowed, and now we have made up our minds to locate on Tobacco Plains, north of here, and go to farming."

A Queer Camp Guard.

The next day we moved about four miles and pitched camp again to prospect. While we were getting ready to go up a little creek, we saw four Nez Perces coming to our camp. We gave them some dinner and then left them in charge of our camp with all our guns and camp outfit scattered around. "The idea" said Ben. Welch, "of leaving our camp and guns in charge of hostiles. The Missoula people would not believe this if we would tell them." But when we returned we found everything as we had left it. Next day we started across the first range, called Grave Creek Pass. It took us three days to reach the boundary of the Main Range. Here we prospected for several days but had no success. Finally we returned to the Indians at Tobacco Plains.

The Killing of White Women.

I went into the Chief's lodge where they were smoking. I asked "How many white women did you kill in Idaho, and where did you kill women and children?" They answered "We burnt one white woman and child on Camas Prairie, unintentionally. She hid herself and child in the upper part of the building. We did not know she was there until the house was in flames and we heard the woman screaming. Joseph Jr., ordered us to put out the fire and we tried very hard to do it. We carried water every way we could but could not put out the fire, so she had to go to her long sleep. There was also another woman and child murdered in White Bird Cañon. We think her husbands name was Emanuel but are not sure. There were four drunken Indians got after her and one of them stabbed her with a knife. We heard that the woman and child were wrapped in a blanket and put inside of their house and that after this was done some of the young warriors who were behind set fire to the house. We did not see the house burn but we heard about it afterward. That is all we know about murdered women in Idaho. We could have killed many more women and citizens but our Chief, Looking Glass, would not permit us. He said only if we were attacked by soldiers, then we might fight as much as we pleased." The Indians denied that Mrs. Emanuel had been outraged.

Another Capture.

At or near Horse Prairie, Looking Glass' brother while hunting captured another white woman. He said she was weeping bitterly when he met her. She asked him to spare her life. He asked her if she was alone. She said "Yes, my husband and children left me without saying a word. I was in the milk house making butter and my husband and children were in the house when they saw the Indian camp moving. They went away without saying a word to me." "The woman," says the Indian, "entreated me to save her. I pointed to where there was thick brush and told her to stay there until all the Indians passed out of sight. She did as I told her." We asked the Indian if he offered to embrace the woman and he said "No, she was crying so bitterly I thought best to leave her alone."

Trouble Among Tribes.

We saw some of the Umatillas and peaceful Nez Perces at Tobacco Plains, who had come direct from Idaho. They claim that some bad white men had killed some of their relations lately, and that in retaliation they had taken his horses. They said they would not have done it but the white man was a horse thief and murderer; if they had done wrong they were willing to return the animals to the owner. They even offered us the animals to send back, but we told them we did not want to meddle in the matter. Took-alex-see-ma has taken charge of the animals. The day I left the Indians moved back towards the East Side of the Rocky Mountains, as the Kootenais tried to master them and flog some of them according to the Jesuit religion, but they could not stand the lash. The Kootenais gave as a reason that the Nez Perces were dancing the White Cockade dance with the Kootenai women, which is in violation of the rules of their religion.

Want to Return.

I think the Nez Perces, some of whom are experienced and successful farmers, will try and become citizens under Her Majesty's government, and take up and cultivate land. As I am informed White Bird and his Nez Perces claim they do not now, and never did, want to fight the whites. If they would be permitted to remain on any of the reserves in Montana or Washington Territory they would like to return and be at peace. They do not want any appropriations or annuities — only a place where they can remain unmolested and make their own living farming and growing stock. They say however, the United States has refused them permission to do this, and that they are now compelled to become British subjects and support themselves north of the line.

Yours Truly,
Duncan McDonald.

From North of the Line.
Some Interesting Items Concerning the Sioux and Nez Perces.
[From *The New North-West* (Deer Lodge, Mont.), Dec. 19, 1879, p. 2, c. 2.]
Special Correspondence *New North-West*.

Fort Macleod, N. W. T., Nov. 21, 1879.
Times are hard here, especially with the red man. There is not a single head of buffalo to be seen and the government will not feed the Indians, so you may form some idea how hard it is for them, and they will not work. A good many citizens have left here with their cattle, complaining that the Indians kill them. Some men have lost largely. Most of the Indians are now toward Bear Paw Mountains, and there is a rumor that the military force at Fort Assinaboine have ordered them off from the Indian res-

ervation through the Indian agent of the Blackfeet. If that is the case British Indians will have a hard time this winter. Even the game is all killed off. The Nez Perces are camped at the Kootenai Lakes living on fish. But we think they will take their blankets off in the spring and commence farming. They are rustling for a living and to my certain knowledge have not yet killed any cattle. After I arrived here I learned from a Nez Perces chief who came direct from the Sioux camp that the head chiefs of the Sioux are holding private councils about the head chief, General Sitting Bull. They want to arrest the General and turn him over to Uncle Sam. The rest want to go back south of the line. They want peace. They are a long distance from here toward Wood Mountains. White Bird is as blind as a bat.

Yours,
Duncan McDonald.

Wintering in the Far North.
How Some of the Nez Perces Were Snowed in and Rescued.

[From *The New North-West* (Deer Lodge, Mont.), Feb. 6, 1880, p. 3, c. 1.]

We received this week from Mr. Duncan McDonald a personal letter which has been nearly two months in coming. It is dated Kootenai Lakes, fifty miles north of Fort Macleod, N. W. T., December 13, 1879. In the course of it allusion is made to the destitute condition of the Indians there, there being no buffalo in that region, and the following incident is related:

"There are ten lodges of Nez Perces here. One day two Indians went after mountain sheep and killed four nearly on top of the highest Rocky Mountain peaks. They were afoot and could not bring them in. Next morning one of the hunters, three women, an old man and a boy started on horseback after the meat. At the foot of the mountain they left their horses and proceeded afoot. When they reached the cache the old man was exhausted and the others nearly so. A terrible snow storm was raging meantime. They took a few pounds of meat and started down the mountain but after traveling a few hundred yards the old man weakened and laid down. They wrapped him up in his one old blanket and buried him in the snow. A half mile further down one of the women gave out, and she too was buried in the snow, the hunter rendering all the assistance he could to the women. Soon after the other two women and the boy gave out and were likewise buried in the snow by the hunter, the storm meantime increasing and the party having no means of making a fire. The hunter then started for camp, reaching there at midnight, and gave the alarm. A rescue party of four at once started, reaching the two women and the boy about daybreak. The hands and feet of the women were some frozen. When the third woman was found she was very badly frozen but still alive. The old man was found curled up like a wolf in the snow drift, with only a thumb and finger frozen. The woman who was worst frozen was put on my back and, with the assistance of the brother of Looking Glass, I carried her down the mountain to where the horses were. She was senseless but was restored to consciousness after being placed in her lodge. This woman is a cousin of Chief Joseph, and when the Nez Perce war broke out owned about 1000 head of horses. She is now poor and badly frozen."

Life in the Far North.
Some Quaint Sketches of Nature and Art — Festivities with Prairie Girls — Godfrey's Cordial.
by Duncan M'Donald.
[From *The New North-West* (Deer Lodge, Mont.), Apr. 2, 1880, p. 2, c. 5-6.]
Special Correspondence *New North-West*.

Just before Christmas our, the travelers', lodge stood on a gravel beach of wash at the base of the highest snowy peaks of the great Rocky Mountains, the backbone of North America. Between two high peaks, about one mile apart, lie the three, bottomless Kootenai Lakes. On the east side, horizontal with these lakes, are the Great Plains of the North-West Territory. Over them the snow is driven wildly by the unceasing winds and man is compelled to curl up in his teepee like a wolf, or be frozen. One of our party, a dyspeptic, went out for a "constitutional" walk. On his return his right cheek peeled off like the skin of a potato.

The Kootenai Lakes.

The first lake is about one and one-half miles long, north and south. The second lake, which feeds the first, is about a mile above — where the stream commences to widen again — is about four mile long and lies east and west. The third one, which is about twenty yards above the second, is about ten miles in length and lies north and south. From the upper end of the third lake to the lower end of the first is about 16 or 17 miles, the three forming a triangle. The thundering Lakes continually splashing against the formidable shores remind us of Old Ocean. These Lakes are about fifty miles nearly due south from Ft. Macleod and are wedged in the timberless, snowy mountains.

Good Fishing Grounds.

The Indians who depend upon these Lakes for fish are the Nez Perces. They have caught fish there weighing from 15 to 30 pounds and 3 to 3^1/2 feet in length. The accounts of the fishing in the Yellowstone National Park are ludicrous to us. If Providence and the National Government would permit a "swap" to be offered we would certainly decline. We got there sturgeon, white fish, brook and lake trout and the noble pike. A fish weighing 30 pounds have been caught with a pitch-fork. Of course such as noble prize could not be taken by any one less blooded than the offspring of a Lord or Duke of Great Britain. This is evidenced by the fact that it was a son of a lord of the realm, by name Hugle who caught the thirty-pounder with a fork, having harpooned him in about three feet of water. On the sides of the mountains surrounding these Lakes we can see the Mountain Goats and Big Horns gazing at us from inaccessible heights.

Precarious Stock Growing.

At the lower end of these Lakes is a trading establishment owned by F. Kanouse. He is also trying to raise stock. He had a considerable number of hogs and chickens, but mountain storms swept down and every one was frozen. He was fortunate enough to save his cattle, but unfortunately the second storm was composed of the Queen's red subjects who slaughtered them. Many a stockman has lost his cattle by the Canadian Blackfeet.

Meeting in the Wilds.

I do not wish to meddle with the religious business of others, but that your readers may understand the religious customs and habits of the far North, I will relate an incident that occurred in December. While lying in the lodge one day, the thermometer marking about 40 degrees below zero, I saw at a distance of three miles a body of men approaching. They were Indians and soon after reached our camp. A tall man came in and extended his hand. We accepted the proffered token of amity, and he informed us he was one of the Mountain Stoney chiefs, named Spital-tall-man. He said "I am starving; can you let me have something to eat?" "Certainly," I replied, "I am willing to help any one in that condition." I then gave him a square meal and presented him with 100 pounds of flour. It was nearly Christmas. The band pitched their camp near ours and Spitah said the Stoneys were great hunters and when the Holy Day came he would make us a present of all the venison we wanted and we would have a big time. The Nez Perces and Stoneys had about an equal number of lodges. One party was Drummers and the other as strong Protestants under the control of John MacDougald, who is a missionary living at Bow River. We awaited anxiously to see their religious festivities and hear their doctrines. The natives built a Medicine Lodge about sixty feet in length where they could have plenty of room to dance. Christmas finally came and we had a grand blow-out in the line of Indian grub. I should have said before we had the big feast that I heard for the first time the doctrines of the

Great Prophet Smohalla.

I had read a great deal about them in the newspapers, the drift of all being that his teachings were in violence to civilization. When the feast was spread on the appichemous ready to eat, the oldest man, an adherent and disciple of Smohalla, rose to ask a blessing from the Supreme Deity, and said: "We believe in a Supreme Being, who made heaven and earth and created mankind. He made the waters and the animals and fish for man to drink and eat. He placed the sun, moon and stars in the sky that we might see, and he covered the earth with grass and herbage that the animals may feed. The Supreme Being has put everything in this world for the good of mankind. To-day is a happy one for us, not only because it is the day Christ was born, but because the whites celebrate this day and enjoy themselves and our leading men deem it best for us to enjoy ourselves on this day as well as others. His dearest words to us are, "Love one another; keep your hearts clean. We must not kill, nor steal, nor lie." He says the young man can select a young woman for a wife if each is suited to the other and they shall live together until death. He says the fathers and mothers should teach the children all good things; that, if we are wicked, when we die no one will mourn or regret us. If we are good we will have sympathy in this world and in the next happy hunting grounds. Now we will feast and sing songs and dance and enjoy ourselves." This is the religion of Smohalla. We accepted its teaching and the mountains echoed our joy.

War Paint Discussed.

We often hear about "War Paint." When an Indian is painted they say he is on the war path. I was born in an Indian country and have Indian blood in my veins, but I never could tell war paint from peace paint. The talk about war paint is ridiculous nonsense, although we frequently hear it said, "I saw an Indian with his war paint on; he is on the war path." Paint is like anything else of an Indian's dress or fancy, and feathers likewise. When city ladies fill the wrinkles in their faces, and wax and paint themselves and put on their fancy, feathered bonnets, and fill their mouths with false teeth, are they on the war path? When a lean, bald-headed, toothless white man puts on a wig, has a dentist fill his mouth with false teeth and his tailor pad his clothes with cotton, and adds a white shirt and brass buttons to win his darling's heart, is he "on the war path?" Certainly not. So with an Indian. Paint is part of his dress. Go into their churches and you will see the Indians painted and feathered. They claim that paint is good for the skin; keeps it from chapping. The red lover wears paint to win his girl's heart just as the white man patches himself up for the same purpose. He wears it alike when Peace sits smiling in her sweetest mood or amid the strife of raging battle. The paint is always the same. When a white man starts out to kill another does he carry a sign that he is on the war path? Do you suppose an Indian does?

An Old Timer Found.

At Fort Macleod we found an old pioneer of the early days in California — Agronauts you call them. Later he was a resident of Missoula. I mean Dan Driscoll. He left Missoula county in 1889 for the Peace River country. Two or three years after we heard he was dead. After leaving Missoula he located near Okanagan Lake; went thence to Thompson's River, B.C., from there via Jasper House to Red River where he lost most of his horses by disease. Then he bought a race horse and came to Fort Macleod last fall. Had some races with the Police but the Red Coats would not give up the money to him. He expects to go across the Kootenai pass in April to Okanagan.

Col. [James F.] Macleod had an increase in his family on New Year's evening. Thanks to Providence it is of that sex to be one of the force to fight old Crowfoot's warriors in case the Dominion Government don't feed the Blackfeet Indians.

The "Proper Thing" at Fort Macleod.

The substitute for whisky at Fort Macleod is composed of Jamaica ginger, Perry Davis' Pain Killer, strawberry water, Cayenne pepper and nutmeg. There are dances from three to five times a week. One night we were invited to attend a party given by a prominent citizen of the town. On entering the Grand Hall

— with dirt roof — we noticed a somewhat cosmopolitan assemblage of people. A Saskatchewan half-breed walked up to us and said, "Pitch in; introduction is played out in this part of the world." We took seats, intending to engage partners after a time. Finally we felt like having a dance and walked over toward the Prairie girls — the true aboriginal occupants of the soil — and proceeded after the methods of Montana to solicit the pleasure of dancing with two of them. They looked at us and shook their heads. We returned rather crestfallen to our seats. A French half-breed walked up to us and said "What is the matter, young men?" We said we had been refused. "Refused! Refused!" he exclaimed; "I've been in this country all my life and that't the first time I ever heard of a girl refusing to dance with a man. Come on boys; I'll get partners for you." He went over to the women, seized one by the wrist and giving her a "yank" that sent her spinning to the middle of the room he furnished one of us with a partner and a moment after another came on the floor the same way. We had no trouble getting partners after we found out the way of the country. All you have to do is to drag them out and they'll dance plenty. The rougher one uses the better they like him.

Fashion Notes and "Permit."

Some people might imagine this is outside of civilization, but they would be mistaken. Ribbons five and six feet long and 8 or 10 inches wide fly around our buffalo girls and some wear them trailing from the top of their well oiled heads to the very floor. If ribbons are a measure of civilization we are *bon ton*.

After dancing we were quietly invited out to take a little walk. Our guide whispers, "We have a little *Permit* left, and it is good stuff." He referred to Permit whiskey, the name coming from the fact that when a man wants some for his own use he has to get a "permit" from Lieut.-Governor Laird and have good recommendations. Not using spirituous liquor I declined but my friend took an elegant drink of the permit and found it was pure water mixed with a little more water.

The Science of Rumology.

At another time we met a man who knew a little about alcoholic chemistry, or Rumology, as it is called. He mixed Cutting's strawberries, black pepper and sugar, added a small quantity of Ginger, Pain Killer, Hair Oil and other liquids — anything so it *was* liquid and boiled it well together. He then called a bull-whacker, told him he had "a little of *the best*" left and if he would raise a subscription among the boys he would let them have it cheap. He had about a half gallon. The b. w. went back to the dance hall, raised $8 and got "the best." Anything in a bottle sells for whisky.

Rum and Religion.

One Sunday some parties went to church drunk. The preacher was singing a hymn as they entered. One man called out, "Can you save me?" The minister quietly answered, "I cannot save you now; it is too late." The unfortunate minister has many hard deals. When there is no Ginger the hearers are few. Again, when the boys have some they club in and march to the church. There were 72 cases of Jamaica Ginger sold at Ft. Macleod, in about two months at $1 a bottle. Such is one phase of life at Ft. Macleod.

A Coal King.

We concluded to travel eastwardly and in about 30 miles reached the establishment of Nicholas Shearan, a contractor who furnishes the government with coal. He also deals largely in dry goods. While there we were very kindly treated by him. Nick is the Coal King of the North-West. He is a hard working man and deserves a fortune in his business.

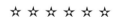

From the North.
A Land of Cold, Snow and Hunger.

[From *The New North-West* (Deer Lodge, Mont.), Mar. 19, 1880, p. 3, c. 4.]

Coal Banks, N. W. T., Feb. 29, 1880.

I am here yet — storm-bound. I went 25 miles down the South Fork of the Saskatchewan River, but my horses were so poor I had to return. I have lost four head already. There is plenty of snow and little of anything else between here and Cypress Hills. I camped on the South Fork a week and all I could see was the sky closing down on the snow — not a beast or bird cheered the desolation. While traveling between this and the mouth of Little Bow river I came across two Cree lodges. The people were all starving. All they had to depend upon for food was the porcupine, and even they were scarce. The poor wretches offered their services to guide me to any place I wanted to go if I would feed them. I was obliged to decline their offer. They offered to trade me the only gun they had, and on which they depended for subsistence, for a horse. They said they would go to Fort Edmonton — about three hundred mile distant — and try to farm in the spring. They had only two porcupines, weighing about eight pounds, on which they expected to subsist while making the journey. Under the circumstances I told them they had better keep the gun and declined to trade. There is no sign of Indians or white men along this river, except the occasional mail carrier. I shipped some flour to Cypress Hills and Fort MacLeod last fall and am trying to get to the former place. I have not seen a letter or newspaper from Western Montana since I came here.

D. McD.

Footnotes

Introduction

1. William S. Lewis, "Spent Boyhood Days at Old Fort Colville," *Spokesman Review* (Spokane, Wash.), April 28, 1929.

Historical Introduction

1. Mary Ronan, *Girl from the Gulches: The Story of Mary Ronan*, as told to Margaret Ronan, ed. by Ellen Baumler (Helena: Montana Historical Society Press, 2003), pp. 155-156.

2. *The Weekly Missoulian* [hereafter "WM"], July 6, 1877, p. 3, c. 2; "The Flatheads," *The Helena Independent* (daily), July 4, 1877, p. 1, c. 6-7.

3. Duncan M'Donald, "The Nez Perces War of 1877," *The New North-West* (Deer Lodge, Mont.) [hereafter "NNW"], Jan. 10, 1879, p. 2, c. 5.

4. Duncan McDonald to L. V. McWhorter, Feb. 1, 1928, box 8, folder 40, Lucullus Virgil McWhorter Papers, collection 55, Manuscripts, Archives, and Special Collections, Holland Library, Washington State University, Pullman, Wash. [hereafter "McWhorter papers"].

5. Joseph McDonald, inteview, March 19, 2015; Camille Williams to Mr. McWhorter, June 21, 1937, box 12 folder 84, McWhorter papers; Camille Williams to McWhorter, undated letter fragment, box 12 folder 80, McWhorter papers.

6. Alvin M. Josephy, Jr., *The Nez Perce Indians and the Opening of the Northwest* (New Haven, Conn.: Yale University Press, 1965), pp. 573-633.

7. Ibid.

8. Angus McDonald to Hiram Knowles, before June 1878, Hiram Knowles Papers, MS 2, box 1, folder 3, Montana Historical Society Archives, Helena.

9. Peter Ronan, *"A Great Many of Us Have Good Farms": Agent Peter Ronan Reports on the Flathead Indian Reservation, Montana, 1877-1887*, ed. Robert J. Bigart (Pablo, Mont.: Salish Kootenai College Press, 2014), p. 239.

10. WM, Aug. 9, 1876, p. 3, c. 2; "Why Indians Abandon the Reservation," WM, Mar. 29, 1878, p. 3, c. 3-4; "An Open Letter," NNW, Apr. 26, 1878, p. 3, c. 6; "Precinct Officers," WM, Nov. 15, 1878, p. 3, c. 2; *Progressive Men of the State of Montana* (Chicago: A. W. Bowen & Co., 1902?), p. 1567.

11. "In Memorium," *Contributions to the Historical Society of Montana*, vol. 5 (1904), pp. 265-272; James H. Mills, "Reminiscences of an Editor," *Contributions to the Historical Society of Montana*, vol. 5 (1904), pp. 273-288;

"Capt. Mills Crosses River," *The Helena Independent* (daily), Sept. 6, 1904, p. 5, c. 1-2; *Progressive Men of the State of Montana* (Chicago: A. W. Bowen & Co., 1902?), pp. 317-318.

12. "The Nez Perces Campaign," NNW, Apr. 19, 1878, p. 2, c. 2.

13. Duncan McDonald, "The Nez Perces," NNW, Apr. 26, 1878, p. 3, c. 5.

14. *Rocky Mountain Husbandman* (Diamond City, Mont.), May 9, 1878, p. 3, c. 2; NNW, May 10, 1878, p. 3, c. 6; NNW, May 17, 1878, p. 3, c. 6.

15. "The Nez Perce Papers," NNW, June 14, 1878, p. 3, c. 2; Duncan McDonald, "Indian Feeling," NNW, June 14, 1878, p. 3, c. 5-6.

16. "En Route," NNW, June 21, 1878, p. 3, c. 1.

17. *The Helena Daily Herald*, June 18, 1878, p. 2, c. 1.

18. Except as noted, this account of Duncan's July 1878 trip to Canada and meeting with White Bird is based on "Notes on Duncan McDonald and John Lebson," Joseph M. Dixon Papers, MS 55, box 99, folder 99-6, Toole Archives, Mansfield Library, University of Montana, Missoula; Duncan McDonald, "The Nez Perces War of 1877," NNW, Mar. 28, 1879, p. 3, c. 4-5; Duncan M'Donald, "White Bird and Sitting Bull," NNW, Aug. 9, 1878, p. 3, c. 4; Jerome A. Greene, *Beyond Bear's Paw: The Nez Perce Indians in Canada* (Norman: University of Oklahoma Press, 2010), pp. 134-153; Canada. Governor General's Office, "Papers Relating to the Nez Perce Indians of the United States, Who Have Taken Refuge in Canadian Territory," Numbered files, RG7-G21, vol 323, file 2001-1, microfilm T-1387, frames 1178-1198, Public Archives of Canada, Ottawa.

19. Duncan McDonald, "Letters from Duncan McDonald," NNW, July 26, 1878, p. 2, c. 4.

20. John Rhone, *Wild Horse Plains* (Plains, Mont.: The Plainsman, n.d.), pp. 19-21; Bud Ainsworth, "Neptune Lynch Family Were First Settlers in Plains Valley...," *Rocky Mountain Husbandman* (Great Falls, Mont.), Aug. 4, 1932, p. 1, c. 1-3.

21. Duncan McDonald, "Letters from Duncan McDonald," NNW, July 26, 1878, p. 2, c. 4.

22. NNW, July 26, 1878, p. 3, c. 3.

23. NNW, Aug. 2, 1878, p. 3, c. 2.

24. "The Return from Exile," NNW, July 19, 1878, p. 3, c. 2.

25. D. B. Jenkins, "The Murder of Joy, Elliott and Hayes," NNW, July 19, 1878, p. 2, c. 2-3.

26. Ibid.

27. "The Hostiles," *The Helena Independent* (daily), July 21, 1878, p. 3, c. 2.

28. C. S. Nichols, "Stevensville Pioneer Tells Interesting Story of the Chase After Chief Joseph's Renegades," *The Daily Missoulian*, May 28, 1916, ed. section, p. 1, c. 1-7.

29. "Pursuit of the Murder Party," NNW, Aug. 2, 1878, p. 2, c. 5; "The Recent Battle on the Clearwater," WM, Aug. 2, 1878, p. 3, c. 3-4.

30. Duncan M'Donald, "An Appeal to Reason," NNW, Aug. 16, 1878, p. 3, c. 4.

31. Ibid.

32. NNW, Aug. 16, 1878, p. 2, c. 1.

33. Duncan McDonald, "'Friendlies' or 'Hostiles,'" NNW, Aug. 30, 1878, p. 3, c. 5.

34. "From Philipsburg," NNW, Aug. 30, 1878, p. 3, c. 4.

35. "Notes on Duncan McDonald and John Lebson," Joseph M. Dixon Papers, MS 55, box 99, folder 99-6, pages 16-19, Toole Archives, Mansfield Library, University of Montana, Missoula; Jerome A. Greene, *Beyond Bear's Paw: The Nez Perce Indians in Canada* (Norman: University of Oklahoma Press, 2010), pp. 118, 135-150.

36. "Notes on Duncan McDonald and John Lebson," Joseph M. Dixon Papers, MS 55, box 99, folder 99-6, pages 19-21, Toole Archives, Mansfield Library, University of Montana, Missoula; Duncan McDonald to Mr. T. D. Duncan, undated, Duncan McDonald Papers, SC 429, vol. 1, p. 35, Montana Historical Society Archives, Helena; James E. Murphy, *Half Interest in a Silver Dollar: The Saga of Charles E. Conrad* (Missoula, Mont.: Mountain Press Publishing Company, 1983).

37. Duncan M'Donald, "The Nez Perces War of 1877," NNW, Jan. 24, 1879, p. 3, c. 4-6.

38. NNW, Jan. 24, 1879, p. 2, c. 1.

39. NNW, Feb. 7, 1879, p. 2, c. 1.

40. NNW, Feb. 14, 1879, p. 2, c. 1; "From Bannack," NNW, Feb. 14, 1879, p. 3, c. 1.

41. Duncan M'Donald, "The Nez Perces War of 1877," NNW, Mar. 21, 1879, p. 3, c. 3.

42. Duncan M'Donald, "The Nez Perces War of 1877," NNW, Jan. 24, 1879, p. 3, c. 4-6; NNW, Jan. 31, 1879, p. 2, c. 1.

43. Duncan McDonald, "More About Indian 'Medicine,'" NNW, Feb. 21, 1879, p. 3, c. 3.

44. Ibid.

45. "A Handsome Present," *The Helena Daily Herald*, Mar. 10, 1879, p. 3, c. 2.

46. Duncan M'Donald, "The Nez Perces War of 1877," NNW, Mar. 28, 1879, p. 3, c. 4-5.

47. NNW, Mar. 14, 1879, p. 3, c. 2.

48. "End of the Nez Perce War History," NNW, Mar. 14, 1879, p. 3. c. 1.

49. Duncan McDonald, "From Over the Line," NNW, Oct. 24, 1879, p. 2, c. 5-6.

50. Peter Ronan, *"A Great Many of Us Have Good Farms": Agent Peter Ronan Reports on the Flathead Indian Reservation, Montana, 1877-1887*, ed. Robert J. Bigart (Pablo, Mont.: Salish Kootenai College Press, 2014), pp. 118-119, 123-125, 140.

51. Duncan McDonald, "From Over the Line," NNW, Oct. 24, 1879, p. 2, c. 5-6.

52. Ibid.

53. Ibid.

54. NNW, Nov. 7, 1879, p. 2, c. 1.

55. Duncan McDonald, "From North of the Line," NNW, Dec. 19, 1879, p. 2, c. 2.

56. "Wintering in the Far North," NNW, Feb. 6, 1880, p. 3, c. 1.

57. Duncan M'Donald, "Life in the Far North," NNW, Apr. 2, 1880, p. 2, c. 5-6.

58. NNW, Mar. 5, 1880, p. 2, c. 1.

59. Duncan McDonald, "From the North," NNW, Mar. 19, 1880, p. 3, c. 4.

60. Duncan M'Donald, "Life in the Far North," NNW, Apr. 2, 1880, p. 2, c. 5-6.

61. NNW, June 18, 1880, p. 3, c. 5.

Index

Note to readers: Duncan McDonald's manuscripts did not always make it possible to distinguish between different Nez Perce with the same names. It was especially hard to distinguish between references to Chief Joseph, old, (c. 1790-1871), who negotiated the 1855 treaty and was the father of the Chief Joseph at the Battle of the Bear's Paw; Chief Joseph, young, (c. 1840-1904), who surrendered at Bear's Paw; and Joseph, the younger brother of the Joseph who surrendered at Bear's Paw. Please use references to like named Nez Perce carefully.